# Managing Subject Access Requests

A Practical Handbook for EVERY Business

By Stephen Massey & Catriona Leafe

**Fox Red Risk Publishing is an Imprint of Fox Red Risk Solutions Ltd (9997987)**

27 Old Gloucester Street, LONDON, WC1N 3AX, UNITED KINGDOM

#GDPRSubjectAccess

978-1-9998272-3-6 (Print)
978-1-9998272-4-3 (Kindle)
978-1-9998272-5-0 (ePub)

# Dedication

We dedicate this book to our families;
those here;
those parted and;
those yet to come.

# Foreword

I am honoured to write this foreword. Not simply because Stephen is a friend and colleague, but because he writes in a very readable, helpful, and practical way.

Data Subject Access Requests (DSARs) are not new. DSARs have been part of data protection law for many years. Some organisations are good at responding to requests, some not so good, and some absolutely awful. There can be many reasons such as poor processes, not enough resources, lack of support in the organisation or staff simply not understanding the basic requirements.

Stephen & Catriona, in their book, gives us a very practical approach. Not only to the simple questions but also to some of the more complex questions and scenarios too. They have sought to help by giving to us, this very easy to read, and practical book. This book should be on the bookshelves of all organisations responsible for conducting DSARs.

I commend this book to you,

Barry Moult
**ICO's Practitioner Award for**
**Excellence in Data Protection 2020**

# Contents

# Table of Figures

# Introduction

## Welcome to the book!

Welcome Reader! Thanks for buying the book (or taking the time to borrow it from someone else!). This book is all about fulfilling someone's right to access by means of a Data Subject Access Request. The right to access is a fundamental right contained within many data protection regulations globally. In particular the EU and UK General Data Protection Regulations. The right to access can often cause headaches for business. Tens of thousands of Data Subject Access Requests are made every month and sadly, many are not fulfilled properly. Many poorly fulfilled DSARs result in complaints lodged with the Data Protection Regulator.

To put this in perspective, in the financial year 2021/22, the UK Information Commissioner's Office (ICO) received[1] 36,343 complaints. Of that number, a whopping 37%, well over a third, related to the right to access. That said, it is also worth pointing out that many complaints raised with the UK ICO were quashed as no infringement was identified. What these complaints (both merited and unmerited) show, is there is significant room for improvement in the way DSARs are handled...and that is why this book now exists.

Data Subject Access Requests can be quite daunting and so we put this book and supporting course together to help those tasked with fulfilling DSARs get through the process as painlessly as possible. In our experience, organisations with little or no training can find the DSAR process a highly resource intensive activity. But, with the guidance in this book, there are lots of nuggets of gold that will help reduce your DSAR burden - and reduce that burden significantly!

But let's get two things out of the way first. Number one. This book assumes **absolutely no knowledge** of data protection, or more specifically, any knowledge of the right to access. It's written for the layperson who needs to deal with data subject access requests – whether that is occasionally, or every day. That said, there is something for everyone, no matter your current level and as such, the book can be used in a number of different ways.

---

[1] ICO Complaints Statistics - https://ico.org.uk/about-the-ico/our-information/complaints-and-concerns-data-sets/data-protection-complaints/

Number two. Whilst this book makes several references to the EU General Data Protection Regulation (GDPR), the contents of this book are not just for those organisations operating in the EU. Many countries around the world have introduced data protection legislation that includes a right to access (e.g. CCPA/CPRA in the USA or PIPEDA in Canada), and many more will do so well after this book has been published. It is likely by the end of this decade that the right to access will be a universal right (with the exception of a handful of countries). The content of this book is, therefore, just as relevant if you're reading in Sacramento, or London, or Johannesburg or down in Wellington. So, if you're in one of the many countries around the world that have (or will have) a right to access enshrined in your laws, this book is still for you!

# How to use this book

If you're new to the Right of Access this book can serve as a full step-by-step guide. Taking the user from theory all the way through to delivering a Data Subject Access Request (and dealing with any potential follow-up). If you're someone who already supports or manages a team who deals with DSARs this book can be used as a supporting reference or, to benchmark your current approach. As a consultant this book can be used as a measure of good practice that can support your advice, or as an auditor it can be used to provide a reference in support of your audit findings. Each chapter covers a specific aspect of the DSAR process and is supported by the Right to Access Fulfilment Model (RAFM) – more on the RAFM later. The chapters are in the order in which the DSAR process should ideally be conducted, and each chapter builds upon the previously covered content. By the end of the book, you will have a solid grounding to then apply the knowledge gained in your own organisation or in a practice environment.

Applying the knowledge learned throughout this book is key to locking in understanding. Fulfilling a DSAR takes more than just knowing the theory. You need to consolidate the theory by applying the knowledge in this book. This can be done in a work-based setting, under the supervision of a more experienced data protection practitioner, or through action-based learning. To facilitate the action-based learned pathway, we recommend enrolling on the accompanying DSAR online course at:

www.foxredrisk.com/dsarcourse.

There you will find even more learning material including video lectures, confirmatory quizzes, and practical exercises. You can even ask us questions too!

# Chapter One - Background & Theory

So, we haven't lost you already...good, good! Here's where things get going properly. The first point of call on our journey to DSAR mastery is to cover the background and the fundamentals underpinning why Subject Access Requests need managing in the first place. Now, you may already be involved in Data Protection. You may be a Data Protection Officer (DPO), you may work in a privacy team, or you may be on the front line dealing with customers on a daily basis - in which case you may already know the basics. Even if you do know the theory already it is still highly recommended you read through this chapter to give yourself a brief refresher. Not just that though, there are also some useful tips in this chapter to help reduce the effort, time, and resource you apportion to DSARs. As mentioned in the introductory paragraphs we will be using European Data Protection legislation as the basis for the theory. If you are elsewhere in the world, it's still worth reading but some aspects may be less relevant. With that aside, let's get started...

## Data Protection Principles

Underpinning the data protection regimes of the UK and the EU are Data Protection Principles. There are seven in total. These data protection principles "embody the spirit"[2] of how lawmakers expect those entrusted with data to act and "lie at the heart" of the UK & EU data protection regimes. The data protection principles are:

Principle one is that all data in relation to the data subject must be processed lawfully, fairly and in a transparent manner. This is known as the **Lawfulness, Fairness and Transparency** principle.

Principle two states that personal data must be collected for a specified, explicit, and legitimate purpose and not further processed in a manner that is incompatible with those purposes. Further processing for archiving purposes, public interest, scientific or historical research purposes or statistical purposes shall not be considered incompatible. This is the **Purpose Limitation** principle. You can't do anything with the data without a lawful basis and you must have communicated this to the Subject, for

---

[2] UK ICO - ttps://ico.org.uk/for-organisations/guide-to-data-protection/guide-to-the-general-data-protection-regulation-gdpr/principles/

example, through your Data Privacy Notice or Data Protection Notice.

The third principle is that the data must be adequate, relevant, and limited to what is necessary in relation to the purposes for which the data is processed. This is known as the **Data Minimisation** principle. This is saying that when you collect data you don't need to be collecting tons and tons of personal data about a data subject if it is not actually relevant to what you are doing. For example, if you're running an online shopping cart and you need to collect information about the customer for the purpose of the transaction you can't ask them random questions about where they went to school or what their thoughts are for the future. You've got to keep it relevant and minimalist.

The fourth principle is that data must be accurate and, where necessary, kept up to date. Every reasonable step must be taken to ensure that inaccurate personal data, in regard to the purpose for which it has been processed, is raised, or rectified without delay. This is the **Accuracy Principle**. Data can and will change over time, for example, you may have a customer that changes address. If you are informed of this in one system, it is your responsibility to make sure that you update your records accordingly. If you rely on that address in a different system, it is incumbent upon you to keep all those other systems accurate. Accuracy is one of the big issues when it comes to Data Subject Access Requests. It is highly likely that the reason you are getting a Data Subject Access Request is because the data you hold is incorrect.

The fifth Data Protection Principle is that personal data must be kept in a form which permits identification of the data subject for no longer than is necessary for the purposes of which the data is processed. Personal data may be stored for longer periods if the personal data will be processed solely for archiving purposes in the public interest, scientific or historical research purposes or statistical purposes. This is known as the **Storage Limitation** principle. In terms of DSARs the storage limitation principle is going to be really helpful in terms of your processing of such requests. If you don't have that much data, or you remove data when it is no longer needed, then the searching, collating, redacting and everything else that goes into producing a DSAR is going to be a lot less onerous. I'd encourage anybody who is dealing with DSARs to make sure that their organisation is fulfilling this principle – it will make your life a lot easier.

The sixth Data Protection Principle is that personal data must be processed in a manner that ensures appropriate security of the personal data. This includes protection against unauthorised or unlawful processing, against accidental loss and destruction or damage using appropriate technical or organisational measures. This is known as the **Integrity and Confidentiality** principle. This principle is going to be helpful in minimising your DSAR volume. If you are an organisation that keeps customer data secure, then it is highly unlikely you are going to end up on the front pages of the major newspapers or on the evening news. As a result you are less likely to have customers coming to you and saying, "I heard you have bene hacked, is my personal data affected?"

The final data protection principle is the **Accountability** principle. This states that the controller shall be responsible for making sure that their organisation adheres to, and is compliant with, all the data protection principles just described: making sure the processing is lawful, fair and transparent; making sure the purposes of processing are limited; making sure that the data collected and processed is minimised; making sure that data is accurate; making sure data is stored for the minimum period necessary; and making sure that data is secure whilst it is being processed. Whilst the likelihood of DSARs dropping to zero is not going to happen, if an organisation adheres to all seven principles, including the Accountability Principle, you will receive far fewer requests. Accountability is such a key principle that we shall be discussing it in greater detail in Chapter Four.

# Data Subject Rights

In addition to the data protection principles which describe at a high level how personal data must be protected, there exists in law, certain rights afforded to each citizen protected by said law. In the UK and EU there exists eight data protection rights. One of which is the subject of this book, the right to access. These data subject Rights are as follows:

The Right to **Portability:**  This means the data subject has a right to transfer certain data from your organisation to another of their choosing and this must be in a machine-readable format.  A good example is energy meter readings that the data subject has collected and provided to their energy company.  The data subject would now like to transfer that information to another organisation to see if they can get a better deal.

The Right to **Rectification:**  This means that a data subject has the right to request that the information an organisation holds is corrected, and this is quite a common reason for people making a DSAR.  For example, if a data subject receives something that is not quite correct - for example a misspelt name, typographical address error or incorrect date of birth - the data subject can submit a DSAR to find out all the different places where this information is held and have it all rectified in one single swoop.

The Right to **Erasure:**  In certain circumstances a data subject has the right to request personal information an organisation holds on them so this data can be permanently deleted.  This is also known as the right to be forgotten.  The request to permanently delete the information may be a follow-on action to the original DSAR.

Rights in relation to **Automated decision making and profiling:**  In some circumstances the data subject has the right to request that automated decision-making or profiling is conducted manually, and the data subject can request information with regards to the decision-making mechanism.  As an example, a data subject may make an application for a credit card or mortgage and the organisation employs an automated decision-making process in order to support that process. This may result in a negative application and the data subject may wish to know why their application has been turned down. The data subject can use the DSAR mechanism to find supporting information before deciding if they wish to take further action.

The right to access: This is the right that is the primary subject of this book. We will look into this right in a lot more detail. But at a high-level legislation such as the General Data Protection Regulation (GDPR) and California Consumer Privacy Act (CCPA) gives the data subject the right to request details of the personal information that an organisation holds on them.

The Right to **Restrict Processing:** A data subject has the right to request the controller or processor halts processing in certain circumstances. For example, a data subject may be aware that their data is being processed and they can use the DSAR mechanism in order to find out what is being processed and why. They also have the right to request that whilst this DSAR is actioned any current processing of their data is (temporarily at least) halted.

The Right to **Object:** This means that a data subject has the right to object to a controller or processor processing their personal data. In these circumstances the controller or processor must stop processing the data unless certain conditions are met. If legitimate reasons cannot be provided as to why the processor is suitable for processing the data then processing must stop. This could obviously create major issues for an organisation and whilst out of the scope of this particular book it is really important to conduct due diligence on any third-party processors.

The Right to be **Informed:** This right encompasses the obligation by a controller to provide fair processing information and typically this is in the form of a Privacy Notice. It emphasises any transparency over how a controller uses personal data, and this is where organisations can get DSARs very wrong. There is an assumption that all that needs to be done is to bundle up a collection of documents into an encrypted zip file and that is it. As we will discover later there are several other things you need to include alongside that personal data.

For those of you who might want a quick and easy way to remember these you can use the mnemonic PREPAROI.

| P | The right to data **PORTABILITY** |
|---|---|
| R | The right to RECTIFICATION |

| E | The right to **ERASURE** |
|---|---|
| P | The right to automated decision making and **PROFILING** |
| A | The right of **ACCESS** |
| R | The right to **RESTRICT** processing |
| O | The right to **OBJECT** |
| I | The right to be **INFORMED** |

*Figure 1 - Data Protection Rights*

So, if this book is concerned with the right to access, why do we even care about the other seven rights? Well you need to keep them in mind. As we get to the end of a real DSAR you may find your data subjects want to exercise one, or more, of these other data protection rights. They may find you hold incorrect data and want it rectified. They may wish to object to, or restrict, the way you process their personal data or and you will need to be ready to deal with these follow-on requests in a timely manner.

# The Right to Access in Brief

In prior sections of this chapter, we briefly touched on the data protection principles and the data subject rights. Let's now get to the specific subject matter of this book – the right to access. Before processing a DSAR, it is important that you understand the right to access in your location. You should be able to tie back your processes to the requirements of a specific piece (or pieces) of data protection legislation. For this purpose, let's have a look at EU GDPR Article 15, which enshrines the right to access in EU law. If you're operating in a different jurisdiction, take a look at your local legislation.

Article 15 states the data subject shall have the right to obtain from the controller confirmation as to whether personal data concerning him or her is being processed, and, where that is the case, access to the personal data and supporting information.

A controller thus has three things to consider:

1. Are they processing data, or not?
2. If yes, then a controller must provide the data subject with the access to the data that it is processing.
3. The controller must also provide supporting information to supplement the personal data that you have provided in the first instance.

Article 15 continues that the following items must be included in a Data Subject Access Request:

- A **copy of the personal data** undergoing processing. Without fee (in most cases) and in electronic form should it be so requested.
- **The purposes of the processing.** The data subject needs to know why you have their personal data and what you are doing with it.
- **The categories of personal data concerned.** For example, if you are processing any special categories such as race, ethnicity, political persuasion, or sexual orientation, this must be disclosed.
- The **recipients or categories of recipient** to whom the personal data have been or will be disclosed, in particular recipients in third countries or international organisations. Put simply, who has the controller shared data with?
- Where possible, **the envisaged period for which the personal data will be stored**, or, if not possible, the criteria used to determine that period. This is effectively your retention period: if you're only going to store that data for six months then this is the information you need to include in the DSAR.
- **The right to be informed**, where personal data is transferred to a third country or to an international organisation, of the appropriate safeguards relating to the transfer. If the data is leaving the jurisdiction of the law that protects it how will its protection continue to be maintained?
- **The existence of data subject Rights.** These are as we've already explained but will need to be included in the supporting material of the DSAR (more on this later).
- **The right to lodge a complaint with a supervisory authority.** In the UK that is the Information Commissioner's Office but depending on which country you're in that may be a different organisation.
- **Where data is not collected from the data subject you must also include the sources where you have got that data from.** For example, you may have received data from a third party or a public source, such as Companies House or the electoral roll, and where this is the case you must tell the data subject where you got their information from. If you got the data from a third party you must give the name of the third party involved.
- **The existence of any automated decision making or profiling.** A lot of this information may already be included in your Privacy Notice and, if this is the case, you don't necessarily need to include it in the DSAR. However, if the information is not included in your Data Protection or Privacy Notice you will have to include this in the supplementary material you provide to your data subject.

- **The right to obtain a copy of the personal data held shall not adversely affect the rights and freedoms of others.** This means a data subject can have a copy of their personal data but that is not at the expense of any other data subject.

So, we know what we need to provide, but how does a controller know a data subject has made a valid Data Subject Access Request? Well, this can be a little tricky. Most data protection legislation is consumer protection focussed. GDPR, CCPA or PIPEDA are no different. The legislation considers a data subject may exercise their right to access in a less than legally formal way. It intrinsically understands the data subject may not be a legal expert who knows how to fully articulate their right to access and so the bar for what constitutes a valid DSAR is pretty low. Article 15 further supports the data subject by preventing organisations from making the process unnecessarily complex or by forcing a data subject to make a DSAR in a particular way (e.g. by physical post or by using a specific web-based form). Communication conveying a DSAR does not need to include phrases or keywords such as "subject access" or "DSAR" or "I am exercising my lawful right to access". If it is implicit the data subject is requesting details about their personal data, it is a DSAR and must be treated as such. No matter who receives the request, and no matter the medium (e.g. letter, telephone, email, social media) it must be treated as a though it was a fully formed Data Subject Access Request sent to the right person in the organisation.

Let's look at a brief example. Say a data subject tweets to a company's official Twitter account the phrase "What do you hold on me?", is this a DSAR? The short answer is yes. The tweet should be treated the same as a detailed request made by an expert data protection practitioner or solicitor on the data subject's behalf. The employee receiving the tweet (whether human or robot) must be able to recognise DSARs, no matter how poorly crafted they may be, and ensure they get passed on to the person who will be able to fulfil the request. This needs to be done swiftly as the clock will then be ticking down those 30 days.

Article 15 also requires that controllers provide DSARs in electronic form should the data subject request the material in electronic form. Similarly, if they want the material in paper form, the controller must also comply with such a request.

There you have it! There is a lot to think about AND all of the above must be provided securely to the data subject within a calendar month - or a little longer if particularly complex. In case you missed it above, the controller cannot charge the data subject for all the effort either. Don't worry though, we will show you how to keep the effort to an absolute minimum! Starting with the next section on reducing the DSAR burden!

# Reducing the DSAR Burden

Before going any further it is a good idea to understand why organisations get DSARs from their customers in the first place. If organisations understand the underlying reasons behind a DSAR they might be able to avoid DSARs altogether. If the DSAR burden can be reduced that is going to make everyone's life a whole lot easier. The fewer DSARs the better! In a recent online interaction with a vendor who sells Data Subject Access Request (DSAR) automation software, they highlighted that organisations across London, UK have seen a staggering increase in DSARs since GDPR went live.

An article in the Yorkshire Evening Post confirms this is not just a London-centric issue.

> *"In Wakefield, there's been a 35 per cent increase in subject access requests since GDPR came in, and staff now have to look through 1,000 more documents for every request."*

It's not really a surprising revelation. The removal, in most cases, of the £10 admin fee and the ability to request the information via electronic means has clearly made the process a lot easier for data subjects. What many organisations are failing to appreciate though is that high volumes of DSARs are a proxy metric for other issues within their organisation. Your customers really don't want a big binder full of their correspondence or screenshots of databases. It's far more likely they are frustrated with some aspect of your company's business practices. In short, if you are struggling to cope with high volumes of DSARs, you don't have a DSAR resource problem, you have either:

- a Service Delivery problem and/or
- a Customer Service problem and/or
- a Data Minimisation problem

If you can fix the issues above it's highly likely the volume of, and time taken to process, DSARs will go down on their own - significantly! Here's why.

## Service Delivery Affects DSAR Volumes

How is your service delivered? Have you ensured your processing is lawful? Are you delivering the service your customers expect? If your service delivery is good, you are less likely to get complaints. If there are problems with service delivery, then complaints will start rolling in and at this stage the DSAR problem is simmering under the surface. It's possible a well-handled complaint could nip the issue in the bud until the delivery issue is fixed but, on the flip side, a poorly handled complaint will cause the issue to escalate into a DSAR quickly...which leads on to how companies deal with complaints,

# Customer Service Affects DSAR Volumes

Some good questions a DPO can ask of their organisation are "What is the training programme for first-line customer service management?" and "Are all customer-facing and back-office staff given customer service training?" I'm not talking about handling Data Protection issues here; I'm talking about how customer-facing employees deal with complaints. For example, when responding to complaints do you give stock answers with little-to-no substance such as:

> *"We take all customer complaints seriously. We are really sorry that you were inconvenienced today however we are unable to help you any further."*

Customers hate platitudes like this. We don't know why companies think this will appease anyone as all this does is wind customers up. It's not the only example. We have countless anecdotes from family, friends, colleagues, and clients about how they made a fairly simple request of a company employee only to be told:

> *"I'm really sorry, it's our policy not to provide that information."*

It's usually NOT the company policy at all. In some cases it CAN'T be the policy as the same information must be provided within a DSAR. It's quite often because the employee can't be bothered to go that little bit further to improve customer satisfaction, or perhaps they don't know how to get the information and/or who to ask. So, what does the customer do in this case...yup...they say:

> *"Well, if you won't give me this tiny bit of information, I will have ALL the information you hold on me."*

You now have a situation in which a small, easily administered task becomes onerous. The DSAR problem is exacerbated when poor service delivery is also causing an increased volume of complaints. By failing to resolve complaints or small requests at the time organisations now have to deal with the subsequent DSAR ... and dealing with a DSAR leads on to how your organisation stores personal data...

# Data Minimisation

When service delivery and complaint management processes have ultimately failed to resolve the customer's issue, the Data Protection Officer's team must now process all the subsequent DSARs. If the organisation has unnecessary complexity in the way it processes customer data then processing a DSAR is also going to be affected by that complexity. For example, if Data controllers and Data processors keep personal data in multiple locations; if employees use their mailboxes like their own personal filing system; if your employees download data and manipulate it in Excel instead of the primary source; or if organisations are keeping records for years longer than needed... well, the organisation has made a rod for its own back. The vendor we mentioned said it took one organisation 21 days to just *discover* the information needed to service a DSAR. That doesn't leave much time (9 days total, so probably 5 workdays) to review and redact that data before passing it back to the data subject using a secure method. If an organisation takes 21 days to discover data, there are clear records management issues that need addressing!

## DSAR Volumes - What can you do?

There are quite a few things that can be done but focus on the actions that will give the most 'bang-for-the-buck'. Naturally, the first and most obvious things to do would be to deliver great service and a customer-centric approach to complaints management. If, however, you don't have these things in place, the next best thing to do is monitor and fix issues at the root cause (don't paper over). Ensure your organisation has the means to monitor the problem. Establish appropriate Key Performance Indicators (KPIs) to measure why customers are making DSARs and ensure this information is fed back to the appropriate management teams who can effect change.

Keep data to a minimum. The less data you have, the less you need to search through and review. Re-engineer databases if necessary. You may find by rationalising your processes for data protection you not only reduce the cost of dealing with DSARs, but also reduce other operating costs too; lower storage, fewer databases to manage, fewer servers to patch, less maintenance. It all adds up. Whatever you do, don't let customer-facing employees blag customers that the "computer says no". Treat customers with the respect they deserve… after all their custom pays for your salary.

## Dealing with Complexity

In the previous section we discussed techniques controllers can use to reduce DSAR volumes, methods that could be used to bring such high numbers down and how to minimise the data held. Whilst those techniques help with overall volumes what happens when a single Data Subject Access Request is itself complex? In this section we will look at the concept of complexity in DSARs. What it is (and isn't) and the techniques available to controllers to help manage complex data subject access requests.

# What is meant by complexity (and what isn't)?

The UK ICO has some guidance on what they consider to be complex. The guidance states the following as complicating factors:

- Technical difficulties in retrieving the information – for example if data is electronically archived.
- Applying an exemption that involves large volumes of particularly sensitive information.
- Clarifying potential issues around disclosing information about a child to a legal guardian.
- Any specialist work involved in obtaining the information or communicating it in an intelligible form.
- Clarifying potential confidentiality issues around the disclosure of sensitive medical information to an authorised third party.
- Needing to obtain specialist legal advice. If you routinely obtain legal advice it is unlikely to be complex.
- Searching large volumes of unstructured manual records NB: This is only applicable to public authorities.

What are **not** considered as complicating factors in a DSAR are as follows:

- High volumes of data involved. Just because a controller holds a lot of data doesn't make the request complex (but can make complexity more challenging).
- Retrieving data from multiple systems. Whilst it may be a complicating factor to retrieve personal data from a specific type of system (e.g., encrypted off-site archives) or personal data held across multiple systems this doesn't make the request complex.
- Reliance on a processor. Whilst material retrieved from a processor may form part of a complex DSAR, the retrieval from the processor itself is not deemed a complicating factor.
- High volumes of Subject Access Requests. Complexity relates to the specifics of a single DSAR. Just because a controller is dealing with a lot of DSARs simultaneously does not make the collective batch of DSARs complex.

An important point to highlight is that even where DSAR complexity exists it does not equate to a de facto exemption. A controller can't withhold information because of these complicating factors. A controller can't respond to a DSAR by stating it was "too hard" to fulfil. A controller must still provide the personal data requested where it is required to do so. All the existence of complicating factors does is give the controller a little more time to fulfil the DSAR.

# Great - but we must still deal with the complexity. Any tips?

As mentioned, controllers must still provide the personal data requested when required to do so by law. They must still deal with all the complicating factors and, whilst the deadline is two months further down the line, the clock is still ticking. With that in mind is there anything controllers can do to make dealing with complex DSARs less onerous? The short answer is yes! Here are some things controllers can do to make their lives easier.

**Review adherence to the DP principles**: As we have highlighted earlier in this chapter the right to access that underpins the DSAR does not sit in isolation. controllers should understand that dealing with a complex DSAR will be more challenging, especially if an organisation is not applying the data protection principles to personal data that may form part of a complex DSAR (or even a simple one!). Make sure that controls relating to purpose limitation and data minimisation are effectively applied. The less personal data held, for example, means reduced effort in the review, in the seeking of advice and redaction stages of the DSAR process.

**Use case management tools**: Let's look at the following scenario. Someone gets a phone call from a data subject and the employee taking the call agrees to do something that has a legal effect on the data subject. An email discussing the issue is sent to someone internally. Somewhere within the chain is a key piece of information confirming what has been agreed. The problem is what was agreed didn't happen because someone went on holiday, or left the organisation, and now nobody can find the paper trail. The data subject insists their version of events is accurate but has no record because the matter was only discussed over the phone. Then, someone in the business takes a view that the data subject must be mistaken, and the data subject now faces some negative effect. The data subject then complains, the company does not uphold the complaint and the data subject then feels compelled to make a DSAR. The email is then found during the searches! A lot of time and effort, not to mention goodwill, has been lost. Had this organisation relied upon case management tools, instead of using email as a filing system, there would have been a formal record of the action to be taken with a unique reference number and a date showing when the issue was resolved (or if it still remained open). We will talk about case management tools a little later in Chapter Five.

**Identify technical retrieval issues early**: Organisations should not wait until a DSAR hits the desk before thinking about how it is going to be fulfilled. Those tasked with retrieval should not be trying to work it out at the time of a request either. Each personal data source should be mapped out. Detailed procedures should be documented to support the retrieval process on each of those data sources including the search nomenclature to be used. If personal data is held in archives, again consider the data minimisation principle, ensure Information Lifecycle Management (ILM) is baked into each data source.

**Develop strategies by wargaming complex case scenarios**: Most organisations have business continuity and incident management plans. A key part of these is the testing component where organisational resilience is evaluated for weakness. The same principle can apply to the DSAR process. Those likely to deal with complex DSARs will benefit from wargaming responses to complex DSARs. For example, if you are in the education sector and regularly need to communicate with legal guardians about their wards, identify ahead of time what should be provided and what would be covered under an exemption? Similarly, if you work in social care and you receive a request for sensitive information about a vulnerable person what needs to be included? When wargaming such scenarios consider how other legislation would interplay with data protection law too. If you're being asked for a pupil record an extension may not apply and you have half the time to provide this data. Get your legal team involved too and brainstorm scenarios that may require specialist advice. Can an opinion be sought ahead of time to stave off delays during a live DSAR? As a DPO you could host regular "What if" workshops to tease out how departments would cope in relevant organisation-specific scenarios. Once you have war-gamed don't forget to integrate findings into your continuous improvement programme and ensure policies, processes and procedures are updated to reflect what was discovered.

**Understand your exemptions and automate redaction**: For organisations dealing with complex DSARs on a more regular basis it's likely the same exemptions are going to apply repeatedly. Where possible create procedures for applying exemptions systematically. Train staff involved in the DSAR process on what exempt material looks like so it can be quickly identified and redacted. Where possible consider the use of redaction software that can automate the process of removing exempted data that appears frequently in searches. Automation of redaction can also be used to support the removal of third-party data.

# Simplify Complexity

Complex DSARs don't have to be complicated, and organisations can simplify the process. Whilst applying the Data Protection principles will be of benefit in the round, mapping your data sources, use of case management tools, wargaming and automation will all help reduce the effort involved in complex DSARs. A word of warning though on extensions. Elongating fulfilment of DSARs by applying an extension could lead to a situation where a higher volume of parallel DSARs exist at the same time. This in itself could become a lot more challenging to manage. The objective should be to implement techniques to process all DSARs as quickly and as efficiently as possible – whether they are complex or simple. Use that extra time wisely! This is not the last word on complexity, we will discuss it further in later chapters...but for now let's summarise what we have learned so far!

# Enforcement

Why should I even care about the right to access? If I just ignore the request is anything bad really going to happen to my organisation? The short answer is that it depends. The potential for high fines has attracted a lot of attention since GDPR arrived in the EU but, in practice, the fines are not the only thing in the regulator's armoury. Regulators have many more enforcement tools available. If we take the UK ICO for example we can see some of these powers are enshrined in local legislation e.g. the Data Protection Act 2018; If you're in a different country, and you're looking at your own data protection regulator, then they will likely have similar powers. It's worth having a look at the relevant regulator website to identify the specific powers available to your regulator. For the purposes of this book the Data Protection Act 2018, or UK implementation of GDPR, gives the UK regulator (the Information Commissioner) the power to issue four types of notice. These notices are:

- **Information Notices** (UK DPA Section 142)
- **Assessment Notices** (UK DPA Section 146)
- **Enforcement Notices** (UK DPA Section 149) and
- **Penalty Notices** (UK DPA Section 155).

## Information Notices

An Information Notice compels a controller or processor to give any information to the Information Commissioner's Officer (ICO) that are deemed reasonable to conduct its functions. The main reason the ICO has this power is so it can conduct investigations. This may be for compliance failure or to investigate a complaint. For example, if the controller fails to honour a DSAR or fails to provide all relevant information the data subject can make a complaint to the ICO. The ICO can then compel the organisation to provide information in order to conduct that investigation and determine whether or not the complaint should be upheld. On receipt of an Information Notice the data controller or data processor can be compelled to provide the information requested by the ICO.

## Assessment Notices

The next power, the Assessment Notice, gives the ICO quite exceptional powers. An Assessment Notice can require a controller or processor to let the ICO come onto their premises and be directed to where documents and equipment are held. The ICO then has the power to examine the documents and equipment, have copies taken and be given explanations as to what those documents actually are. They also have the power to observe processing and interview staff. Such powers could make employees feel very uncomfortable, even if they aren't doing anything wrong.

If employees are doing something wrong then further enforcement action is likely. Even more so if issues are found beyond that detailed in the original complaint – especially if the issues identify system data protection failures!

# Enforcement Notices

The next level up is the Enforcement Notice. This could be issued where a controller or processor has breached one of the Data Protection Principles and the purpose of an Enforcement Notice is to mandate or stop action. Failure to comply with an Enforcement Notice may invite further action and may even move onto the next level which is an administrative fine. Enforcement Notices would usually be appropriate where specific action is needed. The main reason for enforcement in terms of a DSAR is likely to be a failure to meet the rights and obligations that the controller has in terms of fulfilling the DSAR. That could be a failure to meet deadlines, failure to provide information, or failure to acknowledge the DSAR in the first place. As we go through further sections we will highlight the different scenarios which could result in enforcement action.

# Penalty Notices

Where the situation has got to the most serious level we then have the Penalty Notice. The ICO has stated quite clearly that they will reserve this power for the most serious cases where there has been a severe breach of a data subjects Rights. This is typically where the organisation has wilfully, deliberately negligently or repeatedly breached the Data Protection Regulations. As you may know the ICO used to have the power to issue fines of up to £500,000 and they would typically reserve this for the most serious of breaches. Under GDPR this has changed significantly and the ICO can now issue fines of up to 4% of gross annual world revenue. This is a considerable increase in the enforcement powers the ICO has available to them and the stakes for getting a DSAR wrong have increased substantially.

So, there are the four ways in which the ICO, or a supervisory authority in another country within the EU, can enforce the GDPR. By following the guidance and recommendations in this book you will be in a much better position to avoid any of these notices.

# Summary

In this chapter we have reviewed the data protection principles.

- Lawfulness, fairness, and transparency
- Purpose limitation
- Data minimisation
- Accuracy
- Storage limitation
- Integrity and confidentiality (security principle)
- The all-encompassing accountability principle

We then refreshed our knowledge on data subject's rights. They are:

- The right to be informed
- The right of access
- The right to rectification
- The right to erasure, or the right to be forgotten
- The right to restrict processing
- The right to data portability
- The right to object
- Rights in relation to automated decision-making and profiling

We then covered some tips and techniques on how you can reduce having to deal with a lot of Data Subject Access Requests. The key items to consider are:

- Making sure you have excellent service delivery
- Making sure your customer service and complaints management processes are working effectively.
- Most importantly, keeping the amount of data that you hold to an absolute minimum

We then covered what the content of Article 15 contains, and specifically, the things that a Data controller must provide to a data subject. These include:

- The purpose of processing
- The categories of personal data
- The recipients of that data
- The retention periods for the data you hold
- The existence of their data subject rights
- The right to lodge a complaint
- The sources of personal data where they've not been collected by the data subject and;
- The existence of any automated decision making and profiling.

We highlighted that a lot of the content relevant to the right to access should be in your Data Protection Notice so you don't - necessarily - need to include it as an addendum to your Data Subject Access Request but you should always include a link to your Privacy Notice as part of the DSAR response. We then discussed how you can recognise a DSAR, i.e. It can be made via telephone or via email. A person can also make a subject access request via social media, and it doesn't need to include the words subject access to be considered a valid DSAR under GDPR. This may however differ in other jurisdictions.

Finally, we highlighted that one can no longer charge a fee for a data subject access request in most cases, and that organisations typically have 30 days in which to comply with the request. Now we have covered the basics, let's start focussing in on some DSAR theory specifics!

# Chapter Two – Information Governance Primer

In this chapter we will progress from the general data protection theory covered in the previous chapter and move deeper into the specific theory that supports the delivery of the right to access. We will first introduce the concept of Information Governance and how that helps businesses manage the risks and opportunities associated with the information they hold.

Next, we will look at the concept of Data Protection by Design and Default and how systems must be built in a way that support subject access requests instead of hindering! We will then cover Records of Processing Activities (RoPA) highlighting how the RoPA supports the DSAR process. We will briefly cover the Data Protection Impact Assessment (DPIA) and what to consider when processing data in new ways.

We will then move onto a detailed discussion on Internal Roles and Responsibilities. The roles & responsibilities section will discuss who is on the hook, and for what, in the DSAR process. This will help you ensure everyone knows what they need to do to keep the DSAR process running smoothly.

Finally, we will look at the External Roles and Responsibilities and how third parties support your DSAR process. The material in this Chapter will then form the theoretical basis for the practical steps covered in the later chapters.

Let's get cracking!

---

## What is Information Governance?

Information Governance are the processes and controls used to manage information at a controller organisation. In terms of data protection, Information Governance balances the risks associated with personal data with the value that information provides to both the data controller and the data subject. Information Governance helps with legal compliance, operational transparency, and reducing costs; especially those associated with a DSAR. It is worth noting that Information Governance encompasses more than traditional Records Management, it incorporates information security, compliance, data governance, electronic discovery, (which we will talk about a lot in this book), risk management, data storage and archiving. Information Governance also encompasses knowledge management, business operations management, audit, analytics, IT management, enterprise architecture, business intelligence, big data, data science and even finance. There are several Information Governance models out there, including very specific models such as the NHS Data Security Protection Toolkit (which replaced the NHS Information Governance Toolkit), but for this chapter we will be focusing on the Information Governance Reference Model (IGRM) available at www.EDRM.net.

The IGRM is a universally applicable framework for governing information usage in an organisation and is a responsibility model. It helps to identify the stakeholders, define their roles, and then serve to visualise the stakeholder interdependence. Information sits at the centre of the IGRM.

The IGRM model first considers business value. Lines of business have an interest in information proportional to its usefulness. Once the information has lost its usefulness, the business often loses interest in keeping the data accurate and up to date. This, as we know, is a breach of the data protection principles but an all-too-common practice.

The model requires the business to assign a value to its information assets. By defining the value the legal department, the DPO and the other second line governance functions can provide the appropriate systems and controls. Information Technology can also ensure they have appropriate systems in place to manage that data.

Legal, Records Management, and the DPO also have responsibilities and typically provide the governance & oversight for their organisation.

The IGRM underscores that it is the Legal department's responsibility to define what to put on litigation hold. However, where a DSAR is concerned the DPO should have input into the litigation hold process (there will be more on litigation hold later in the book).

Records Management have responsibility to ensure that regulatory obligations are met, including decisions on what to retain and archive, and how long for. In the UK and EU, the Data Protection Officer has tasks listed in article 38 of GDPR. These three stakeholders (Legal, Records Management and the DPO) all have a significant role in how and when companies can dispose of data.

Whilst not a governance role IT is also a key stakeholder. IT is chartered with the efficient management of information systems under their control. IT essentially leans on Legal, Records Management and the DPO to be specific about the IT department's duties regarding the company's information. IT must know what their duties are and where those duties end. IT stores and secures information under their management, but they are typically under huge pressure to increase efficiency and lower costs, and that may often lead to corners being inadvertently cut. Governance & Oversight is therefore critical in ensuring that an appropriate balance is struck. One of the most valuable aspects of this model is it highlights that without collaboration and solid collaborative governance, IT may never know what information has value, or what duties apply to that specific information.

OK, you may be thinking it's great that I now know what information governance is and how it works but why is it important? Put simply, if a controller establishes a consistent and logical framework for employees to manage personal data through a solid Information Governance framework, responding to a DSAR should be relatively pain free.

# Data Protection by Design and Default

controllers must be able to demonstrate how they have designed their business systems containing personal data, whether electronic or manual, so that data protection and security are baked in.  You must be able to provide evidence of how you assess the potential risk to data protection and security, what controls you have put in place, and that those controls are being effectively monitored throughout the life of the system.

Not all data protection legislation has Data Protection by Design and Default, but UK and EU GDPR does. The requirement is enshrined in Article 25 which states:

> *"Taking into account the state of the art, the cost of implementation and the nature, scope, context and purposes of processing as well as the risks of varying likelihood and severity for rights and freedoms of natural persons posed by the processing, the controller shall, both at the time of the determination of the means for processing and at the time of the processing itself, implement appropriate technical and organisational measures, such as pseudonymisation, which are designed to implement data-protection principles, such as data minimisation, in an effective manner and to integrate the necessary safeguards into the processing in order to meet the requirements of this Regulation and protect the rights of data subjects."*

What this basically means is that you, as the controller, must put in place controls and safeguards that protect the data subject's rights and respect the data protection principles.

It is beyond the scope of this book to go into major detail as to what controls should be in place for specific personal data processing systems, but, in terms of the right to access consideration should be given to, but not limited to, implementing the following controls:

- **Search Capability**: How will operators of a system be able to find data on a specific data subject without accidentally including data on another (e.g., someone with a similar name, or someone who lives at the same address?)
- **Right to access Self-Service**: Can the system be designed in such a way that the data subject can access their own data without needing to make a support request?
- **Encryption**: How is personal data protected so that it cannot be accessed by a third party without authorisation
- **Access Management:** Who is permitted to see personal data and how is this access controlled and audited?

If you're finding it hard to process DSARs, because you can't find or extract the data, it maybe you have not implemented data protection by design effectively.

# Record of Processing Activities (RoPA)

It's pretty hard to pull all the personal data your organisation holds together if no one knows where the data resides. Data may start in one system but could be copied, repackaged, and transmitted to hundreds of different systems in the blink of an eye. Organisations must know how personal data is processed in their organisation and where. In the EU this requirement is laid down in Article 30 of GDPR. It requires organisations to maintain Records of Processing Activities (or RoPA for short). Article 30 states amongst other things that:

> *"Each controller and, where applicable, the controller's representative, shall maintain a record of processing activities under its responsibility."*

When it comes to subject access requests accurate records can make life a whole lot simpler. If you know where to look half the battle is already won. Let's have a quick look at the items your records of processing must contain:

- The name and contact details of the controller
- The purpose of the processing
- A description of the categories of data subjects, and the categories of personal data
- The categories of recipients to whom the personal data has been, or will be, disclosed to, including recipients in second and third countries, or international organisations.
- Where applicable, any transfers of personal data to a third country, or international organisation, including the identification of that country, or international organisation.
- Where possible envisaged time limits for the erasure of the different categories of data - this is your organisation's retention policy.

- Where possible a general description of the technical and organisational security measures

It is not only the controller who needs to maintain a record of their processing activities. Article 30 also goes on to say that:

*"Each processor and, where applicable, the processor's representative shall maintain a record of all categories of processing activities carried out on behalf of a controller"*

This should contain the following:

- The name and contact details of the processor, or processors, and each controller on behalf of which the processor is acting, and where applicable, of the controller or the processors representative, and the data protection officer.
- The categories of processing conducted on behalf of each of the controllers.
- Where applicable, transfers of data to a third country or international organisation, including the identification of that third country or international organisation, and any necessary safeguards.
- A general description of the technical and organisational security measures they have in place to protect the controller's data.

Article 30 goes on to say that those records, of both the controller and the processor, must be in writing and must also be in electronic form – you cannot just have a paper record. The controller or processor must also make those records available to supervisory authorities whenever they are requested (in the UK this would be the ICO). The one exception to this is that records do not need to be kept by an enterprise or organisation if they employ fewer than 250 people. This "get out" however, does come with a caveat:

*"...unless the processing that organisation carries out is likely to result in risks to the rights of the data subject".*

If your organisation falls below the threshold of being required to maintain a record of processing activity it still makes sense to keep a record voluntarily. This record will make life so much easier when conducting tasks such as a DSAR. Having accurate records of processing activities will make managing data protection compliance so much easier.

# Data Protection Impact Assessment (DPIA)

In order to ensure that you have the right to access baked in by design and default, it's vital you use a process to assess the impact of your data processing from the outset. In data protection parlance this will often manifest itself as a Data Protection Impact Assessment (DPIA). Some people may also know this as a Privacy Impact Assessment (PIA) – Hi Americans!

At a high level the DPIA process looks at the way in which personal data is to be processed (note the tense, it must be done before you start doing the processing), and then overlays how data subjects' rights and freedoms may be impacted. If the risks to the rights and freedoms are too high then compensating controls must be put in place – or in some cases the processing may not be permitted at all.

The Data Protection Impact Assessment process must require the identification and assignment of a System Owner first. The System Owner must be a competent person who has the power to make funding and governance decisions relating to that system and the data it contains. This is because the system owner will be accountable for protecting EU citizens' rights.

When conducting a DPIA a section will be dedicated to assessing which data protection rights may be engaged by data subjects. In the case of the right to access the assessment would be whether a data subject can make a request for the data held. If such a request can be made then a further assessment should be made as to how that right will be fulfilled. A similar approach should be applied for all data protection rights..

More often than should be the case organisations pay lip service to the DPIA process. Sadly, the DPIA is treated as an afterthought, only produced after a system has already gone live with the appropriate capabilities missing. Ensure the DPIA is well embedded in your organisations as one of the first documents completed when implementing a new system. That way, when someone does make a DSAR the system has the necessary search and extraction capability and is ready to go!

# Roles and Responsibilities

A key part of ensuring that the Data Subject Access Request process goes swimmingly is to make sure that everybody in the organisation knows exactly what their roles and responsibilities are. In this section we will look at the Data Protection Officer (DPO), information security, Legal including procurement, the IT team, and in particular system owners, business owners and employees. Finally, we will look at the leadership team, because as we already discussed in Section One, accountability is a keystone principle of data protection and without it the DSAR process is going to hit some hurdles.

## Internal Roles and Responsibilities

The **Data Protection Officer (DPO)** has a considerable role in the DSAR process because they are providing the primary governance and oversight. One of the key tasks the DPO will have responsibility for is the creation of a data protection policy and ensuring that this policy is communicated throughout the organisation. They will also need to coordinate DSAR training, not just for employees, but for all the roles mentioned above. In addition they will need to advise system owners and process owners about the DSAR processes and procedures. It is not the responsibility of the DPO to write the processes and procedures, but they should be working hand in glove with the system and process owners to ensure the processes are appropriately fulfilling the requirements of the right to access. That might involve a process of system owners writing their procedures and then submitting these to the DPO; or they could look at the Data Protection Policy and go through each of the requirements to make sure they have them covered in the processes and procedures. It is, of course, the responsibility of the DPO to be accessible to the data subject and the regulator. For those of you who may not already know, Article 38 – The Data Protection Officer (Paragraph 4) states that:

> *"Data subjects may contact the data protection officer with regard to all issues related to processing of their personal data and to the exercise of their rights under this Regulation"*

A DPO needs to make sure that they are sufficiently resourced to respond to these queries and questions should a data subject make contact. This includes Data Subject Access Requests and any follow-up questions that data subjects may have about the processing of their data. To ensure the smooth processing of DSARs the DPO must ensure that the record processing for the organisation is maintained. As mentioned earlier in this chapter, even if an organisation is not required to do so under Article 30, we would still recommend that all DPOs instil upon their organisation to maintain these records. For the data subject the DPO has a key role to play in ensuring that the 30-day deadline to meet the DSAR is met.

**Information Security** is usually headed up by a **Head of Information Security** or a **Chief Information Security Officer (CISO)**. This department is a key ally for the DPO and should be a helpful resource in the DSAR process. Here's how... firstly, they can support DPO in the e-Discovery process. Information Security has similar goals to the DPO in that they need to know where data, especially personal data, is located across the corporate network and beyond. If Information Security doesn't know where data is located keeping all that data secure will be impossible! Secondly, Information Security can support data minimisation efforts by ensuring systems and data are securely decommissioned at end of life.

Information Security can also support the DPO by providing advice on secure transmission methods for DSAR material when it ready to go to the data subject. Information Security will play a key role in vendor due diligence in ensuring the vendor's security controls are appropriate and effective. In addition a DPO could seek to leverage the existing third-party risk framework by adding in specific data protection questions.

In terms of system access Information Security can review access management controls for weaknesses and solid access management controls are essential. DSARs will require one or more employees to have access privileges that permit extraction of data from secure systems. Information Security can ensure the correct access is provided, and that the data collected remains secure outside the system. Subsequent to a DSAR, when the process has been completed information security can provide recommendations on how to securely delete and dispose of the residual data when no longer required.

**Legal** are well placed to support the DPO in the e-Discovery process. Bearing in mind legal professionals typically have a lot of training in discovery they will be able to advise an inexperienced DPO on the techniques required. Legal will also have a key role in ensuring that processor contracts facilitate the right of access, so if that's your in-house legal counsel, they can make sure there are standard contract terms and that the whole process accounts for the 30-day deadline. Obviously processors need to have shorter deadlines in order for you to then take that material in and start processing it yourself for redaction etc. Legal needs to make sure that those SLAs are appropriate and there are appropriate penalties involved if they are not met. Legal will be able to advise you on the legal hold process and any statutory record retention period, for example, HR records need to be held for a certain period in countries by law and the same applies with accounting and financial records.

Legal will also be able to advise you on the legal validity of any proposed exemptions. It's always worth having that conversation with them if you're unsure rather than putting yourself in a sticky wicket and having that overturned at a later date. They may also be able to advise on any potential legal locations of disclosure and your company responses. Whilst you don't want to appear to the data subject as being guarded, or your communications being unnecessarily filled with legal speak, equally you don't want to accidentally create liability where no liability exists. Where there is any doubt in anything that you're about to communicate with a data subject I'd encourage you to check it over with your legal team and they should be able to advise you accordingly.

**Information Technology**, and in particular **System Owners**, are really important because they are maintaining the system day to day. They are keeping the system security patching up to date, upgrading the system as and when required, and doing health checks to make sure that data integrity is maintained. Information Security has a lot of responsibility in support of the right of access. They are going to support the DPO in the e-Discovery process and make sure people can get at the data they need. The System Owners need to ensure that the systems are designed to support the right of access, bearing in mind the deadlines and multiple requests that may be required. System Owners must ensure that system security is maintained so that data integrity, availability and confidentiality are protected. In addition, IT will be responsible for working with the business to make sure that when data is no longer needed it is securely removed from the systems and, in doing so, supporting data minimisation. Finally, like everyone else, they need to make sure the system can deliver a DSAR within 30 days.

Every single **employee** in an organisation has a critical role to play in the DSAR process. The primary responsibility for all employees in your organisation is to know how to recognise a DSAR. Employees also need to know they must communicate a DSAR to the DPO or privacy team as soon as possible and ideally within the same business day. Remember you only have 30 days, so every minute is critical when you're pulling together potentially large volumes of data. In the day-to-day course of their work employees need to ensure the data they use remains accurate and up to date, for example, if a customer comes in with a change of address employees need to make sure that this is updated in each system where that address is recorded. Employees must also ensure that data is processed lawfully. Bear in mind that a DSAR may pull in data that identifies unlawful processing and there could be legal implications for the company if they are acting without a legal basis. All employees need to make sure the data they use is minimised. This could mean ensuring they don't download multiple spreadsheets and systems of records to perform ad hoc queries and then not tidy up the data afterwards – although to be honest, they shouldn't be doing that anyway! Finally, like everyone else, it is critical that all employees ensure that, where they are responsible for supporting the DSAR, the request is fulfilled within 30 days.

The final group of people, **your organisation's Leadership team**, are critical to ensuring the DSAR process goes swimmingly. It's not just leadership at the top level, this is the leadership at all levels from your **Junior Managers** all the way up to your **Directors,** and then the **Board** level themselves. The first action is to ensure there is an appropriate tone from the top. The senior management, and every management layer below it, must be positive about the fact that this process needs to be complied with. They must visibly demonstrate that management commitment. They also need to support the DSAR process with appropriate resources; making sure that systems can be designed with the right of access in mind, and then all the way through to ensuring that there are enough resources to process any DSAR that may come in.

They must also empower the DPO and ensure the DPO is not undermined when trying to do their job. Examples of how the DPO might be unintentionally undermined could be through failing to provide appropriate resources to support the DPO's work, in terms of checking systems and complying with DSARs, or not being appropriately vocal in support of the data protection programme within the organisation.

A key action the leadership team can take to demonstrate their ongoing management commitment is to require, and act upon, DSAR Key Performance Indicators (KPIs) and Key Risk Indicators (KRIs). A good example of a KRI would be how many DSARs are being requested in any month? This KRI provides a risk indicator that there may be other processes in the business failing e.g. service delivery or customer service. An example of a KPI would be number of DSARs that are fulfilled outside the 30-day deadline? In a well-oiled process, this should be zero. There are others you may wish to include such as how many exemptions are being applied (and which ones are most common)? How many DSARs result in litigation? How many DSARs result in a request to rectify inaccurate data, or to remove data that should no longer be in place? Metrics will be discussed more later in the book but the key message for management is that they need to be actively engaged in ensuring the organisation is meeting its data protection obligations.

What should now be apparent is that it's not the DPO's responsibility to ensure the DSAR process operates effectively. Leadership, the Legal Department, Information Security, System Owners, and, well, every single employee. Everyone in the organisation will have a role to play, that's why making sure everyone understands their roles and responsibilities within the DSAR process is essential.

## Processor Roles & Responsibilities

In the previous section we spoke about the roles and responsibilities of internal stakeholders, now we will look at the roles and responsibilities of a Data processor. The relationship between a controller and processor must be governed by a contract. First, we look at how a processor can support the DSAR process and what their responsibilities are. If we look at what GDPR says about this relationship we can get a good starting point. Article 28 is a specific regulation and states: -

> *"Where processing is to be carried out on behalf of a controller, the controller shall use only processors providing sufficient guarantees to implement appropriate technical and organisational measures in such a manner that processing will meet the requirements of this Regulation and ensure the protection of the rights of the data subject"* [7]

In simple terms the above means a controller can only use processors who have demonstrated they can comply with GDPR. This means that with respect to the DSAR process they must support the controller to deliver the DSAR material to the data subject within 30 days. It does not mean that they have 30 days to put the material they hold together and supply this to the controller. As a controller this means you need to assure yourself that the processor, both at the beginning of the relationship, i.e. before you sign the contract - and then thereafter – is capable of delivering a GDPR compliant service. This assurance activity may be achieved during monthly or quarterly service management meetings, or as part of a specific Data Protection Audit

So, what responsibilities should a processor have regarding the DSAR process, and how are these applied?

**The processor must only process data as per the written instructions of the data controller.** The processor cannot take that data and use it in any other form. It is critical the processor understands this as any additional processing is still subject to the right to access. Should the DSAR material highlight unlawful processing you as the controller could end up in hot water!

**The processor must keep the personal data that the controller has provided to them secure.** This means the processor must have sufficient technical and organisational controls to keep data secure until such time that a DSAR is made. This will include (but is not limited to) controls to recognise DSARs when made; appropriate data retention controls to minimise DSAR effort; tools to support searches; and tools to support the secure transmission of data to you as the controller.

**The processor must meet DSAR specific Service Level Agreements (SLA).** A good rule of thumb that a controller should consider using is the 1/3 – 2/3 rule. The regulatory deadline to deliver a DSAR is 30 days, The controller should give the processor a 1/3 deadline of ten days to deliver the material, and a further 1/3 deadline, or SLA, to deliver any follow up material, for example, if any data or supporting information is missing. controllers should be aware that collection is only the first stage. There are numerous other stages that you must go through - for example duplication, redaction, and correction - and all those things take time. If there are any issues or items that need to be followed up you still need to make sure that they can be completed within the 30 day deadline. Additionally, in order to provide supplementary information that a data subject might request, for example the meaning of a specific field on a database table, it's really useful to make sure some form of Glossary or supporting information is included. We will talk about supporting information in a further section so look out for that later on.

**A processor must have in place processes to support the other data subject rights.** Remember the DSAR is often a gateway process. The data subject has submitted a DSAR to find out what information you hold on them and they may choose to exercise further data subject rights. For example, in a previous section we spoke about the right to object, the right to be forgotten, the right to restrict processing, or the right to have the data rectified. All of these things should also be conducted under SLAs. When a data subject has exercised their right the controller can then give confirmation, within a reasonable timeframe, that their rights have been adhered to and upheld as per the request.

**Be prepared to provide supporting evidence when requested.** It is important for a Data processor to understand that Article 28 (paragraph 3h) states that the processor is contractually required to:

> *"...make available to the controller all information necessary to demonstrate compliance with the obligations laid down in this Article and allow for and contribute to audits, including inspections, conducted by the controller or another auditor mandated by the controller." [8]*

For example, controllers often conduct data protection audits. During this process a controller will review the processor's data protection processes to identify any potential compliance issues. The Data processor in these situations must make sure that the controller is provided with relevant material in order that the audit can be conducted effectively, and the processor must provide evidence when requested. In most cases organisations will already have a confidentiality clause within their contracts meaning issues of confidentiality should be a moot point … but it doesn't stop people trying it on! There is an age-old Latin phrase that is really important: *Caveat Emptor.* This translates as "buyer beware". In short, always be wary of a potential processor who isn't willing to be transparent about their data protection compliance because it's likely there are other issues at play. .

# Summary

The core focus of this chapter has been to set the scene for the rest of the book's practical chapters. We then moved back into the General Data Protection Regulation and discussed how Article 25 "Data Protection by Design and Default" assists in reducing the effort of collecting DSAR material. How Article 35 Data Protection Impact Assessments can support the assessment of new systems to ensure right to access controls are baked in from the outset. We also looked at how and Article 30 Record of Processing Activities (RoPA) can be a valuable resource in identifying where to focus resources tasked with searching for DSAR material.

Finally, we looked at the key roles and responsibilities across an organisation, and external to it, highlighting how each have their part to play in supporting the right to access. Let's now move to the next chapter where we will introduce the Right to Access Fulfilment Model.

# Chapter Three – The Right to Access Fulfilment Model (RAFM)

In this chapter we will introduce the model that will ensure your organisation can process DSARs effectively and consistently. What is this model we speak of? This model is the Right to Access Fulfilment Model (RAFM). It's a thing of beauty! It describes conceptually all the components of the DSAR process and how they interact. This chapter will introduce the model but then each subsequent chapter will break down a component and show you how to turn them into operational processes.

Before we describe the RAFM in any detail, we feel it is important to discuss the model's origins. We will therefore spend some time discussing another model first. The model from which the RAFM was inspired – the Electronic Discovery Reference Model (EDRM) – The EDRM is also a corker of a model in its own rights but doesn't fully encapsulate what is needed for DSARs and that is why the RAFM was born!

But why do we even need a model? Models are a shorthand that help simplify complex processes. They aid in communicating a set of related concepts concisely. DSARs can be complex and so a model is a very useful way of breaking through this complexity. There are a lot of moving parts within a DSAR and so a model helps us visualise how each part of the process interacts with each other. Models aid in capability assessment and continuous improvement. When a process is not working in one area, a model can aid in analysing where an issue downstream may be causing problems downstream (or vice-versa). Models can also be built upon, modified, and made better too. The RAFM would never have been conceived if it weren't for other people creating models such as the EDRM. Praise be to models! Ok, a bit of hero worship on the nature of models but hopefully you get the gist that without a model it would be more challenging to convey quickly how the DSAR process works. We hope that the RAFM will quickly convey how a DSAR works from start to finish in one simple diagram. Now, we know why models are important let's now look at the EDRM and how that inspired the RAFM...

## Electronic Discovery Reference Model (EDRM)

It wouldn't surprise us if the primary reason you're reading this book is because you are struggling to deal with DSARs in your organisation. You want to find some guidance to make your life easier. You were probably thinking surely there was a framework already in place for Data Subject Access Requests?! set of steps that a lay person could follow that meant nothing was missed?  Is there another group of people who deal with similar issues on a pretty regular basis, and have they already designed such a framework? Could an average person, in an average business, learn from this group of people? Well, it turns out there is a group of people that can help. These people already deal with every stage of the Data Subject Access Request process – they don't call it a DSAR process though, they call it e-Discovery.

Who are these people?   Paralegals, Lawyers, Solicitors and Barristers. These keen legal minds deal with discovery of documents all day long - and that is pretty much at the core of what a Data Subject Access Request is. A DSAR is essentially a set of steps that deals with personal data discovery and its presentation.

Because the legal profession deals with the data discovery process so frequently it just so happens there are several models for data discovery. One of those models is the Electronic Discovery Reference Model (EDRM)[3].

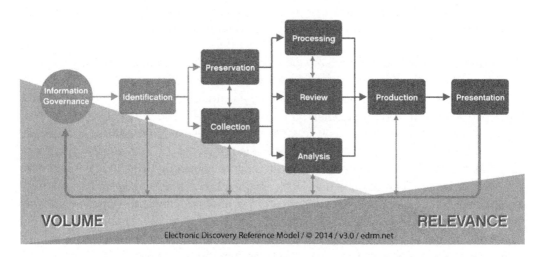

*Figure 2 - Electronic Discovery Reference Model (EDRM)*

The EDRM is a conceptual model that itemises the processes that should be taken to ensure electronic discovery is conducted in a legally defensible manner. The EDRM was first proposed in 2005 and is now well established as a model for electronic discovery. The EDRM consists of nine stages as presented in the diagram above. These stages are Information Governance, Identification, Preservation, Collection, Processing, Review, Analysis, Production and Presentation. Describing the EDRM in any great detail is not within the scope of this book but you can read all about the model and the wider project by going to EDRM.net.

---

[3] EDRM (EDRM.NET)

What is surprising, given the ICO complaints statistics we presented in the opening chapter, is that very little work has gone into developing a model that supports the fulfilment of Data Subject Access Requests specifically. Such a model would be extremely helpful in ensuring DSARs were managed in a manner that provides the data subject with the information they need in an efficient manner. Such a model could materially reduce the burden on controllers and thus reduce the likelihood of a data subject making a complaint to the ICO. Well, we looked around and couldn't find anything so, rather than lament the lack of such a model, we created one. We are very proud to present to you, the reader, the Right to Access Fulfilment Model (RAFM).

# The Right to Access Fulfilment Model (RAFM)

The Right to Access Fulfilment Model (RAFM) was inspired by the efficacy and simplicity of the Electronic Discovery Model (EDRM). The RAFM does to the right to access what the EDRM does to e-Discovery. It aims to help anyone – not just DPOs or Privacy Professionals - work through a Data Subject Access Request in a logical, consistent, and repeatable manner.

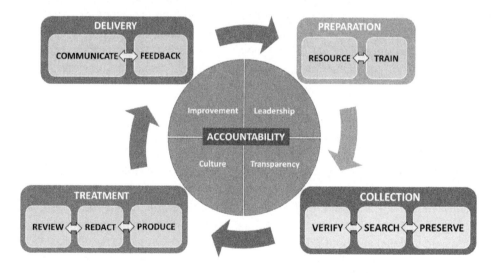

*Figure 3 - Right to Access Fulfilment Model (RAFM)*

In a similar way to the EDRM, the RAFM represents a conceptual view of the end-to-end process. The RAFM is a universal model that can be applied to supporting the right to access in any number of jurisdictions. Whether you're operating under GDPR in the EU or UK, POPIA in South Africa, CCPA in California or, LGPD in Brasil, the RAFM is a model that, if applied correctly, will allow your organisation to demonstrate accountability in relation to upholding a data subject's right to access. The RAFM is a universal model. This means an organisation operating in more than one legal jurisdiction, with some local tweaking here and there, can operate a single set of core processes to deal with the right to access. Equally so, a processor operating anywhere in the world could develop processes to support this model and thus serve controllers in whichever data protection jurisdiction they operate.

As is depicted in the figure 3, the RAFM is broken down into four distinct phased components of Preparation, Collection, Treatment and Delivery, with a hub component of Accountability. Each phase follows on from the previous in a chronological order. Each phase, however, contains iterative sub-processes. The sub-processes are iterative in nature because an output created in one sub-process may require a further work in a separate sub-process before moving to the next phase.

For example, material submitted for review in the treatment phase may not have been redacted correctly and the material may require more, or less, redacting before it is resubmitted for review. Searches performed at the collection phase may identify a significant amount of personal data and may warrant a controller asking a data subject if they would be willing to be more specific with their request.

The four phased components of the RAFM are bound to an overarching **Accountability** "Hub". Accountability is a fundamental principle of good data protection governance. It is only logical, therefore, that accountability encapsulates the RAFM. Accountability manifests itself within the model in four ways – leadership, transparency, culture, and improvement. The accountability components will be discussed in more detail in Chapter Four.

**Preparation**: The preparation phase has two iterative sub-processes and aims to ensure an organisation has effective resources to fulfil DSARs and, in addition, that those resources are effectively trained. The resource and train sub-processes are iterative because as employees rotate in they will require training, and as processes change and develop training will need to be updated with employees then being trained in the new material. For example, if a new case management tool were to be deployed those operating that tool would need to be trained in its use. The preparation phase will be discussed in detail in Chapter Five.

**Collection**: The collection phase has three iterative sub-processes – verify, search, and preserve. The collection phase aims to collect the material requested of a data subject in the most efficient manner possible. The first sub process, verify, seeks to ensure the request has been validated in terms of content, scope, and the identity of the data subject. The second sub-process, search, seeks to ensure the requested material is found, potentially across many systems, and is complete. The third sub-process, preserve, seeks to ensure that any material identified in the search is protected from deliberate or accidental destruction or alteration. The latter part is particularly important should a data subject make a complaint to a regulator as a controller would then be required to defend their processes. Once completed the material is then moved into the treatment phase. The collection phase will be discussed in detail in Chapter Six.

**Treatment**:   The treatment phase has three iterative sub-processes – review, redact and produce. The treatment phase aims to take the data collected in the collection phase and reduce this down to a final subset of material. The final subset of material is achieved by conducting a review to identify duplication, third party content and exempted material. The reviewed material then enters a redaction phase where exempt material is removed. Redacted material is reviewed again before a final redacted subset is approved for production. The production sub-process then takes that final set of material and packages it up with any relevant supporting information ready for delivery to the data subject. The treatment phase will be discussed in detail in Chapter Seven.

**Delivery**:   The delivery phase has two iterative sub-processes – communicate and feedback. The delivery phase aims to take the production ready subject access 'pack' and deliver it securely to the data subject in a manner that allows the data subject to easily access the material. The delivery phase also aims to make the provision of feedback to the data subject, and other relevant stakeholders, as efficient as possible. Furthermore, feedback could include applying other data subject rights arising from the DSAR, such as a rectification request or a request to restrict processing, and finally, communication may include communicating with the Data Protection Authority in the event of a complaint...but hopefully not! The delivery phase will be discussed in detail in Chapter Eight.

So that's the RAFM in a nutshell. A simple model that will help you visualise the various processes that go into fulfilling a Data Subject Access Request. Four phases with iterative sub-processes that, if implemented effectively should make dealing with even the most complex DSAR a doddle. Well, maybe not a doddle but definitely easier than it may have been!

# Summary

Chapter three introduced the Right to Access Fulfilment Model (RAFM). It's origins in the Electronic Discovery Model (EDRM) and the RAFM structure itself. The key components of the structure are the central 'Accountability' hub and the four iterative phases of preparation, collection, treatment, and delivery. Accountability is central to the RAFM as without strong leadership, transparency, a positive data protection culture and, a desire for continuous improvement, the rest of the model will be challenging to deliver effectively. Each phase is iterative to ensure even the most complex DSAR can be supported with the least amount of effort. Each phase contains sub-processes that must all be completed before moving on to the next phase – some sub-processes may need to be repeated depending on the level of complexity associated with a particular DSAR. When all phases are completed, the DSAR can then be closed...and then it's on to the next DSAR I'm afraid.

Now that the RAFM has been introduced and described at a high level, we shall now look at each component of the RAFM in more detail and more importantly how to turn the model into operational processes. As has been mentioned several times in this chapter, accountability is key to getting right to access correct. With that in mind, our next stop, chapter four. is all about accountability!

# Chapter Four – Accountability Phase

*Figure 4 - Accountability Phase*

From this chapter forward we will take the Right to Access Fulfilment Model (RAFM) and turn it into operational processes that can be implemented in your organisation. As briefly mentioned in the prior chapter, the RAFM has 4 phases (preparation, collection, treatment, and delivery), encapsulated within an overarching accountability component. Accountability is a core data protection principle. In some legislation, e.g., GDPR, the principle of accountability is explicitly enshrined in law. Suffice to say, without accountability, it is highly unlikely an organisation will be able to adequately demonstrate compliancy with all the relevant data protection legislation that affects their business operations.

Accountability engenders trust. When a data subject sees an organisation upholding their rights, they are more likely to trust that organisation with their personal data. Where trust is eroded, through a lack of accountability, the likelihood of data subjects invoking their right to access is certain to increase. The key takeaway from this chapter is this – **get accountability right and data subjects will make less DSARs.** The less DSARs made, the less overall effort will be required in upholding the data subjects' right to access. It really is that simple – but what does it take to adhere to the accountability principle in relation to the right of access?

Let's find out…

# Leadership

Without leadership very little happens. This is just as true with data protection as in any other business-related task. But what is leadership? Leadership in business is part art and part science. Leadership is a holistic set of concepts that allows an organisation's leadership team to determine a strategy, and then deliver on that strategy. Leadership is not about ensuring a strategy is delivered at any cost. Leadership is the ability to manage risk and take appropriate action when needed. Leadership requires the ability to take people on a journey and to ensure every part of the business is pulling together to achieve common objectives.

Common objectives for most businesses are to improve customer satisfaction, sustainably grow their customer base, reduce costs, and increase profitability. Good data protection supports all four! Where customers feel an organisation is not processing their personal data lawfully they will become unsatisfied very quickly. Prospective customers are more likely to engage with your organisation if you are not repeatedly in the national press because of privacy and security issues. Getting data protection right reduces costs in several ways, for example, reduced storage, increased efficiency, and reduced incidents. All of these aspects combined ultimately lead to increased profitability.

So, what does good data protection leadership look like? A good starting point for organisations is to seek guidance from their data protection authority. In the case of the UK Information Commissioner's Office (ICO), there is a comprehensive accountability framework that covers "the foundations of an effective privacy management programme". Organisations could also look to align to a relevant standard such as ISO 27701. Within the ICO's accountability framework there are some key issues to consider in terms of demonstrating good leadership.

The leadership issues we feel are important to consider first are:

- Ensuring the most senior level of management have overall responsibility for data protection.
- The establishment of oversight structures or committees chaired by a member of the senior management team.
- The monitoring of data protection metrics. Senior management should review key data protection indicators of performance and risk and take swift and effective action where appropriate.
- There should be appropriate tone from the top. Senior management must consider data protection as a core part of their decision-making processes.
- Ensure appropriate resources and budget are available to support data protection initiatives.

An organisation that demonstrates leadership by implementing these four items effectively will have a sound foundation to support effective delivery of Data Subject Access Requests. If done really well those DSARs should be a rare occurrence too!

# Transparency

One of the first questions we ask when a controller or processor comes to us with a novel and innovative way of processing personal data is this: -

> *"What do you think the impact to your company's reputation would be if this activity was reported on the front page of a national newspaper?"*

The reason we ask this question is simple. There should not be anything an organisation is doing with personal data that would be embarrassing should the underlying personal data processing be reported on the 6-o-clock news. An organisation should be completely comfortable explaining what they do with personal data. In short, they must be comfortable with processing personal data in a transparent manner. Where an organisation is uncomfortable with transparency it's quite possible the processing may be unlawful.

When it comes to the right to access transparency is an extremely helpful tool. When organisations are transparent up front it's less likely data subjects will feel the need to ask you what information you hold on them. More simply, they won't need to ask because they will already know. If, however, you are not transparent, and your processing activities are exposed in a hard-hitting documentary - which then goes viral – it is more likely a barrage of subject access requests are coming your way in the very near future!

Getting transparency right should not take a lot of effort. By following a few key steps organisations can ensure they provide data subjects with all they need to know. These steps are:

1. Ensure employees know they must only process personal data lawfully and transparently. They should know to seek advice from their Data Protection Officer before processing data in a manner not previously assessed.
2. Ensure you publish an easily accessible privacy notice. Changes to processing must be reflected in updated versions and communicated to data subjects before the new processing commences.
3. Ensure your privacy notice is written in plain language at a reading age suitable for your target audience (i.e., if your service is for children, the content of your privacy notice must be understood by children).
4. Ensure employees can explain to data subjects how the organisation processes their data and the underlying lawful bases.

An organisation which implements these four items will have incorporated a high level of transparency into their data protection regime.

# Culture

Culture is a nebulous term and is understood differently by different people. For the purposes of the discussion in this book we will be looking more specifically at organisational culture. Organisational culture is widely discussed in academic research and the definition we will use is that organisational culture is "a set of shared assumptions that guide what happens in organisations by defining appropriate behaviour for various situations"[4]. Organisational culture can be more concisely described as how an organisation gets things done.

Organisational culture will thus play a core role in data protection compliance. If there is a shared assumption that data protection does not matter, employees are more likely to pay lip service to upholding the rights of data subjects. Poor organisational culture can occur both accidentally, negligently, and deliberately.

Poor culture could occur deliberately. A senior manager could be speaking to a more junior member of their team and say something like "don't tell the DPO about this, they'd block what we're trying to do" This then tells the junior member, who is likely more loyal to their line manager than the DPO, that it is ok to hide things from the DPO. The practice of hiding things from the DPO then becomes the standard operating procedure and the DPO only finds out about an issue when something has already gone wrong. This practice can be pretty toxic and the more senior the person doing it, the more widespread the toxic behaviour can become.

Poor culture could occur negligently. An example of negligent dispersal of culture could be a manager not checking what their team is doing with personal data. Another could be not thinking through the data protection issues within the tasks they have been assigned. A member of their team may ask if they could apply something new and innovative with a large personal dataset. Without really thinking about the wider implications of the request the line manager simply says "yes, let me know how you get on". Another team member sees the work of their colleague and then decides to expand on this work but doesn't speak to their line manager before doing so. They try out some other ideas with the same data, including sharing the data with a third-party advertiser. Unfortunately, the line manager was not made aware of these other 'innovations' and before they do find out a Subject Access Request is made. The subsequent collection of data will then reveal a considerable amount of unlawful processing to be disclosed to the data subject.

Poor culture can also occur accidentally. Management at all levels can make off-hand comments without fully understanding the impact their comments may have. Imagine a situation where a senior manager jokingly says something like "We've got the data

---

[4] Responding to Organizational Identity Threats: Exploring the Role of Organizational Culture (Ravasi & Schultz, 2006)

protection police coming this afternoon for a death by PowerPoint session, I wish I had some way to get out of it". Whilst not intended, the comment may be interpreted that data protection is of low importance to the manager and should be avoided where at all possible.

Whether deliberate, negligent, or accidental, poor organisational culture can be pervasive. It can spread very quickly within an organisation and, if left unchecked, can lead to highly toxic practices. If your organisational culture is poor, data protection compliance will likely be a casualty. If data protection compliance is poor, you can bet your house and first-born child, that there will be an impact in terms of an increased volume of Data Subject Access Requests.

Getting organisational culture right is not easy. It's very difficult and it is not something the DPO can do on their own. But, by raising awareness of the impact poor organisational culture has on your organisation's data protection compliance, hopefully you, the reader, can influence and nudge your organisation in the right direction. Consider some of the following as discussion points with your senior management:

- How effective are senior management at communicating the need to comply with data protection requirements?
- How well understood are each employee's role and responsibilities?
- What happens when someone doesn't comply? Are there consequences? How are employees rewarded when they do the right thing?
- Is doing the right thing easy?

The last point in the list, making doing the right thing easy, can make a significant impact when attempting to drive positive change in an organisation. DPOs should collaborate with the business to identify data protection tasks which are onerous, tasks which are complex and tasks which are frequently left incomplete or left to the last minute. Where possible the DPO should then analyse those tasks and identify opportunities for improvement...and improvement is exactly what we're going to talk about next!

# Improvement

Every Data Subject Access Request submitted to your organisation will have its own nuances and complexities. Some of these nuances may be related to the type of data subject (e.g., a child). Some may be related to your mission (e.g., healthcare). Many requests will have some unique aspect, something your organisation has not come across before – perhaps something the authors of this book haven't seen before. Whilst complexity and nuance exist, every DSAR received will also have similarities. Similar challenges will be faced in each of the four phases of the RAFM, similar questions will be asked by data subjects and. the same system will be difficult to search. The same exceptions will need to be applied, the same material will require redaction and the same standard communication will need to be provided to the data subject. Whether complex or straightforward, each of these examples, and many others, are opportunities to streamline your processes, enhance efficacy and increase efficiency. Making these enhancements can be best achieved by ensuring continual improvement is at the core of your data protection regime.

Continual improvement is the act of incorporating incremental changes to the way you approach a task with the aim of making the underlying process, product, or service, better. There are several frameworks which focus on the topic of continual improvement e.g., Kaizen, Six Sigma and Lean, but a detailed discussion on any specific models is out of the scope of this book. At a high-level continual improvement models contain the following similarities:

- Improvement is based on data.
- Improvement is gradual or incremental.
- Improvements are usually low-cost.
- Improvement is locally driven (i.e., by employees doing the work)

Unlike culture, implementing a continual improvement regime is not that difficult, and it's even easier if you can get culture right. As discussed, improvements are low cost, can be made incrementally and you as the process owner can often make improvements with little to no resource. In fact, if done well, you should free up resources to use elsewhere.

A final point …don't underestimate the power of continual improvement. It's very easy to end up in a state of constant firefighting and stay there until you burn out. Even if there are a lot of fires to put out make time to focus on improvement. Some fires may burn a little brighter or a little longer whilst you fix things but, those gradual improvements, will lead to less fires to fight overall.

# Summary

The key focus of this chapter was to investigate in more detail how the principle of accountability fits into the right to access fulfilment model. Firstly, we looked at how leadership encompasses every part of a business, what good leadership looks like and how sound leadership supports the effective delivery of DSARs.

Secondly, we examined the importance of transparency and why it is such a crucial tool within the right to access. We considered why an organisation that has a transparent data protection regime is less likely to be bombarded with Data Subject Access Requests and considered key steps that an organisation can take to act transparently.

Next, we explored organisational culture. Organisational culture plays a fundamental role in data protection compliance. Three ways in which poor culture could occur were highlighted – deliberately, negligently, or accidentally. We considered how poor organisational culture can spread quickly and can unintentionally have a negative effect on the volume of data subject access requests an organisation may receive.

The final section of the chapter looked at improvement. We discussed that whilst all the DSARs an organisation receives will be unique in some respects, each will also have similarities. We considered how these similarities provide the opportunity for improvements to be made to your processes whilst also increasing efficiency and effectiveness.

# Chapter Five – Preparation Phase

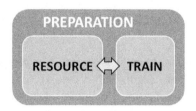

Figure 5 - Preparation Phase

There is an old adage that says proper planning and preparation prevents poor performance. It's never been so true as than when it comes to the Data Subject Access Request process. In this chapter we will walk through the preparation steps of the Right to Access Fulfilment Model (RAFM). We will highlight the items to consider when ensuring an organisation is prepared to meet its right to access regulatory deadlines in its specific jurisdiction.

The two sub-components of the RAFM preparation phase are **Resource** and **Train**. In the resourcing section we will look at where resources need to be allocated. This section will not only look at the resources within the DSAR process itself, but also how resourcing in other areas can help minimise the overall effort across the wider organisation. The resourcing section will look at resourcing in terms of both people and the tools needed to support delivery in all phases of the RAFM.

In the training section we will look at the training needs of an organisation for each of the RAFM phases. _Everyone_ in the organisation will need some form of training relating to the right to access. This training will need to be periodically updated as things change, and people move in and out of roles. We shall therefore identify who needs to be trained, in what, how often, and by whom.

## Resource

From a practical perspective, resourcing must be one of the first things to consider when implementing the RAFM – if you don't have the necessary resources to fulfil DSARs then little is going to get done! If DSARs are not fulfilled, the most obvious consequence will be complaints from data subjects to a data protection regulator. In this section we will look at what resources are needed to support the DSAR process. This includes the library of documents you will need and the tools and equipment that make up your DSAR processing environment. But first, up we need someone to steer the boat...

## Who Owns the DSAR Process?

So, who exactly is running this show? Who actually owns the Data Subject Access Request process? We know the controller's leadership team are accountable and the Data Protection Officer will certainly play a part in the process, but who is responsible for all the day-to-day tasks detailed in this book? You may be immersed in this material because you have been 'volunteered' but are you the right person for the job? Like many questions of organisational structure, the answer will depend on factors affecting the specific organisation. There is no fixed answer. Let's have a look at a few different options.

One option could be that the Operations Manager (or Head of Operations or Chief Operating Officer) role owns the process. The primary advantage of this role owning the process is that it should aid in ensuring that appropriate resources are made available and that those who need training attend. The primary disadvantage is, at least initially, this person may not have the expertise to set up such a process. This is not necessarily a barrier. The Operations Manager would just need to procure assistance from either a data protection officer or an external data protection consultant to things implemented and then work with their DPO to monitor ongoing effectiveness of the implemented DSAR process. Generally, this is our preferred option.

Another second option could be to split the ownership of the DSAR process into categories of data subjects and assign ownership accordingly. For example, a Customer Services Manager might be given ownership of DSARs related to customers and the general public whilst the HR Manager may be assigned ownership of DSARs relating to future, current and past employees. The primary advantage of this approach is that each area can develop processes that are more tailored to their operational focus whilst the primary disadvantage may be that they don't necessarily own all the sources of data related to the requests made. For example, the HR may not have access to all the emails and instant messages of the department an ex-employee was employed. Similarly, a Customer Services Manager is highly unlikely to have access to all the different places customer data may be located (e.g. CRM, email, finance system etc.). If an organisation is not large enough for an overarching head of operations, this would be our next-best ownership model.

A third option could be that the IT Manager (or Head of IT or Chief Information Officer) role owns the process. The primary advantage of this approach is that the IT Manager is likely to have [indirect] access to all the systems where personal data is held and will usually have technical resources and access privileges within their team to carry out the relevant searches. The primary disadvantages are again the lack of control over individual business area resources to support the process and the requirement for whomever is assigned the role to have significant expertise on each aspect of the DSAR process as it relates to all the different types of data subject. Generally, this is not a preferred model. Business Units can often see IT as a 'dumping ground' for such tasks in order to get it off their desk. What can then happen is that the business then fails to support the person in IT coordinating the DSAR because they are not "on-the-hook" if the DSAR deadline is missed.

An often – ill-advised - option is that the Data Protection Officer owns the DSAR process. The advantage of the DPO owning the process is that they will have significant knowledge in relation to all aspects of the DSAR process. The two main disadvantages would be that the DPO would not have operational control of the various resources that are involved in the DSAR process and being involved in the operational process directly would likely become a conflict of interest when viewed alongside the DPOs duties to monitor compliance with data protection legislation. Whilst it may seem like a good idea, we generally do not recommend this approach. These are some options, but you may find another option works better for your organisation. Whichever option you choose, the key takeaway is the owner will need support, resources, and training to implement an effective DSAR process.

# Ownership & Joint Controllers

In jurisdictions like the UK and EU there is the concept of a Joint Controller. Joint controllers jointly determine the purposes and means of processing and so that means they are also jointly accountable for ensuring data subject can effectively exercise their right to access. Whilst this book will primarily focus on DSARs from a single controller perspective, we wanted to highlight that if you're operating in a joint controller environment there are four primary factors to consider when setting up your DSAR processes.

**Division of responsibilities**: Joint controllers need to decide a DSAR process and then who will do what within that process. We strongly recommend that this process is documented and, whilst not a regulatory requirement, it's worth considering whether it is appropriate to make it contractually binding.

**Transparency**: The joint controller relationship needs to be transparent to the data subjects. It also needs to be clear to the data subject how they can exercise their data protection rights. There should not be a situation where those acting for one controller just bounce the data subject over to the other controller or vice versa. The information that the data subject needs should be clearly stated in both controllers' privacy notices and a single notice if this is more appropriate.

**Access to data**: Joint controllers will need to agree how each controller is to access and process the DSAR material that is jointly controller. There should also be a process for jointly agreeing which exemptions apply to the material and what should happen in the event of a differing interpretation of what exemptions do and do not apply.  Another aspect to consider in terms of data access is that the data subject's personal data may be processed in part under a joint controller relationship and in full by just one controller. There will need to be processes to ensure that any data not covered by a joint controller relationship is not inadvertently shared to the other controller.

**Communication**: Joint controllers should agree how to communicate to the data subject. If templates are to be created to support the process, who will own and maintain the templates. Joint controllers should also determine whether there will be a single point of contact and how communication with the data subject made to one controller is shared with another.

# The Right to Access Corpus

Like any well implemented business activity it's good to have things written down and sketched out. This section will describe the set of documents we think will be useful to have in your library. We have split the documents down into five different categories. The categories are:

- Policy
- Procedures & Guidelines
- Records of Processing Activities (RoPA)
- Communications Material
- Audit Trail

Let's have a look at each document type in detail…

## Policy

Before discussing what right to access requirements must be documented in a good data protection policy, it is worth discussing why policies are key documents for organisations. Anecdotally, many organisations write policies as a tick-box exercise, or cut and paste templates from the internet, without considering whether the content is fit-for-purpose for their own organisation. However, those who cut and paste from the internet maybe don't realise their policies could be requested by the Regulator in the event of a complaint or personal data breach. The content of an organisation's policies can be a strong indicator of systemic compliance issues. If you recall when it comes to regulatory enforcement, evidence of systemic non-compliance will likely lead to harsher penalties. The following list highlights some key questions to ask about how your organisation creates and implements its policies:

- Is there evidence of mapping legal, regulatory, and contractual requirements against the policy content? (e.g. requirements map)
- Is there evidence of stakeholder engagement prior to each revision of the data protection policy? (e.g. policy drafts circulated to key stakeholders for review and feedback)
- Is there documentary evidence that management formally approve policies? (e.g. meeting minutes)
- Is there documentary evidence that policy requirements have been communicated to everyone in the organisation? (e.g. an all staff email).
- Is there documentary evidence that policy requirements have been incorporated into business processes? (e.g. references to policy requirements in departmental procedures)
- Is there documentary evidence management have sought confirmation that business processes are compliant with the policy requirements? (e.g. monthly compliance metrics or internal audit reports)
- Is there evidence of structured periodic review of policy content? (e.g. an annual policy review report)

If you find the answer to one, or more, of the questions is no, it may highlight systemic compliance issues that need to be urgently addressed. For the sake of brevity however, this book assumes the controller has in place an effective policy framework that covers policy creation, approval, review, and publication and all are operating effectively. So, whilst we won't cover policy frameworks and how a data protection policy would be approved, we will cover two different approaches controllers can take to incorporate the right to access requirements into their organisation's policy framework. We will also suggest some appropriate policy wording.

The first approach is to create a standalone right to access policy. For organisations operating in multiple jurisdictions this may be a suitable approach, as each jurisdiction may have slightly different requirements in how the right to access is applied. A stand-alone policy could contain standard policy requirements but also include jurisdiction specific appendices to cover regulatory differences.

The second approach is to incorporate right to access policy statements into a section of your data protection policy. This approach would be more appropriate where your organisation typically operates in a single jurisdiction and is only required to comply with a limited set of regulations that impact the right to access. It would also be a good approach for smaller organisations who want to limit the amount of policy documents they need to manage and keep updated.

Whichever approach you take there are some important policy statements to include in your organisational policy. The following statements are the requirements we would recommend are included:

- A Process for fulfilling Data Subject Access Requests shall be documented and maintained.

- Process Owners shall ensure those processing data understand how to identify a Data Subject Access Request
- Data Subject Access Requests shall be recorded in a register owned by the DPO
- Data Subject Access Requests shall be completed as soon as possible and in no more than 30 calendar days
- Data Subject Access Requests shall not incur a charge.
- Data Subject Access Requests shall be processed electronically if this is requested by the data subject.
- Reasonable steps shall be taken to verify the identity of the data subject prior to providing access to their personal data.
- System Owners shall ensure appropriate resource is made available to support Data Subject Access Requests
- Reasonable steps shall be made to seek the permission of third parties prior to including their information within an access request. Where permission is not provided, the DPO shall be consulted to determine whether data should be provided or redacted.
- Requested information shall be communicated to the data subject securely.

You should note from the above that these statements state a requirement but do not state "how" each requirement is to be met. The "how" is not something that should be placed in policy. This would increase the effort needed for senior management to review policy documents, but more importantly means every time a process changes, e.g. a step becomes automated, the policy would need to be reapproved before the policy could go live. This would materially, and unnecessarily, hinder productivity. Stating *how* something should be done will be included in the next set of documents we discuss - procedures and guidelines.

## Procedures & Guidelines

Procedures and guideline documents are just as important as your policies. They help to ensure that business activities are completed in a consistent and efficient manner. Ideally, they will also ensure that everyone understands their specific roles and responsibilities within the processes too. A procedure lays out the steps those involved in a process must follow, whilst guidance gives advice on areas where there is flexibility to adjust an approach. In a well-oiled process procedures and guidelines should complement each other.

From a DSAR perspective, procedures and guidelines should clearly demonstrate the current approach to meeting the right to access policy requirements you have determined and had approved by management. There should be a clear mapping from policy requirement to each of your procedural documents. For example, if we look at the final policy requirement that "*Requested information shall be communicated to the data subject securely*" this means that in practice there must be a written "*secure transmission*" procedure that documents the steps needed to send all the DSAR material securely to the correct data subject. An encryption guidance document could then compliment the secure transmission procedure by listing the current secure cryptographic techniques that are approved for use in your specific organisation.

As you may note, and in a similar approach to documenting policy, separating procedural steps from guidance will reduce the amount of time spent maintaining documents that don't change too often.

## Record of Processing Activities (RoPA)

As mentioned earlier in the book (in Chapter Two), the Record of Processing Activities (RoPA) will be a very useful document when fulfilling DSARs. This is because it lays down in one document all the places Personal Data can be found within your organisation. In particular, having an accurate and up to date RoPA will be a blessing when coordinating search activities, especially if your RoPA can be filtered around common DSAR scenarios, e.g. the ability to filter by customer, employee, patient etc. So, whilst UK/EU GDPR may not necessarily mandate it for your specific size of organisation, we still recommend you create and maintain a RoPA.

## Communications Material

The successful fulfilment of a DSAR is highly likely to hinge on good communication. Get communication right and most data subjects will be happy, get it wrong and the effort involved could double (if not triple!). Your communication effort will be fourfold. There will be internal communication to gather material. There will be communication with your processors to collect information they hold. There will, of course, be communication between you, the controller, and the data subject and there may also be communication with regulators too.

We won't dwell too much on what communication material is needed at this point as this will be discussed in greater detail in Chapter Eight. Suffice to say though, the more communication you can anticipate and prepare for, the more efficient your DSAR process will be.

## Activity Records

No, this is not another paragraph about the RoPA duplicated to increase the word count of the book! What we're talking about here is essentially a record of the activities conducted to fulfil the DSAR. Another way to describe these would be an Audit Trail. Although we don't like to describe activity records this way as they are so much more than proving what you have done and when. Yes, they obviously help demonstrate each step in your process has been followed, but they also help you analyse the individual steps of your DSAR process to identify areas of improvement. For example, if you are failing to meet the 30-day deadline to respond to a data subject's request, what is the root cause? Is it the searches are taking too long to come back? Is there so much legitimate material that means redaction is an arduous task?

Whatever the reason, keeping records for assessment later will create an invaluable dataset - because even if you make the 30-day deadline now, would you still be able to make the deadline if the volume of DSARs increased by 10%, or 20%, or 200%? Making refinements each time should mean your process becomes lightning fast and super-efficient, in turn freeing you up to do other things. We would even go so far as to recommend analysing performance right from your first DSAR to see what could be improved in every subsequent request thereafter. Activity records don't need to be complicated. A simple line In a spreadsheet with "Reference", "Activity", "Time Started", Time Finished" and a "Comments" field is more than enough. If this can be automatically derived from case management software (more on that in the next section), then even better!

OK, now we know what documentation we need, let's move onto tools and techniques!

## The DSAR Processing Environment

The DSAR Processing Environment is the term we will use going forward to describe the collection of tools that are used to support the DSAR process. This section will describe the tools that will aid you from the moment you receive a Data Subject Access Request to the moment you successfully put it to bed.

| Tool | (A) | (P) | (C) | (T) | (D) |
|------|-----|-----|-----|-----|-----|
| Case Management | X | X | X | X | X |
| Discovery / Search | | | X | | |
| Encryption / Hashing | | | X | X | X |
| Redaction | X | X | | X | |
| Secure Communication | | X | X | | X |
| Secure Storage | | X | X | X | |

| | | | | | |
|---|---|---|---|---|---|
| Secure Destruction | | | | X | |
| Knowledgebase/Wiki | | X | X | X | X |

Accountability (**P**) Preparation (**C**) Collection (**T**) Treatment (**D**) Delivery

*Figure 6 - Processing Environment by RAFM Phase*

It's worth clearing something up first - before someone says this section is overkill. Not all these tools are required to fulfil a DSAR. In many cases you may not need any tools at all. This section is written to cater for a set of scenarios, up to and including, the most complex cases a Data Protection professional may face. Cases where a practitioner may be faced with challenging or complex issues, or significant volumes of requests that need managing in parallel. The tools mentioned are deliberately vendor agnostic but, where a particular product is mentioned, the authors do not in any way endorse the product. We strongly advise you draw up a list of requirements, hopefully based on the advice here, and then follow your organisation's procurement processes to identify the tools suitable to your particular circumstances. At a high level figure six displays the tools and how they relate to each phase of the RAFM.

Should you decide to purchase any of the tools discussed we recommend using the procurement tool 'MoSCoW'. MoSCoW determines what you 'Must have' in a system; what you 'Should have' in a system; what a system 'Could have'; and what a system 'Won't have'. By clearly defining your requirements in this way you can avoid being dazzled by vendor solutions that offer lots of bells and whistles and a fancy interface, but don't actually provide the much-needed core functionality. To keep this book concise, we will focus discussion on the 'Must have', and some 'Should have', items. With that in mind let's have a look at each of the tools a Data Protection professional may need in a little more detail.

## Case Management

Dependent on the size of your organisation there may be many people dealing with multiple systems, and they could be processing hundreds of thousands of records. Processing all those records and putting only the relevant information into a DSAR pack will need coordination. At the core of your DSAR processing environment you're going to need something that can collate and track everything that's going on across all the different RAFM processes. If you don't want to get yourself into a complete muddle, get yourself a Case Management tool.

A case management tool is pretty much what it says on the tin. It will keep all the information related to a DSAR in one place so that you can keep track of what has, and has not, been done. Knowing the status of a particular DSAR in relation to what could be hundreds of consecutive DSARs could prove essential in preserving your sanity!

There are several case management tools available. Some are very specific to the process of managing a Data Subject Access Request where others are more generic. Hopefully we can show you that you might already have such a system in place within your organisation, but before we get to that, let's talk about the criteria needed in a case management system.

The first thing your case management system needs is a way to ingest when a Data Subject Access Request is made. Now, we know data subjects can make requests by any method they feel comfortable with, and we can't force a data subject to use a specific way that we want them to. That said, if you can provide data subjects with an easy way to make a DSAR there is a good chance it will be used and that's also going to make your life easier as well. A very simple web-based form on your Privacy Notice will be beneficial in making sure that DSARs get to the right person as quickly as possible, as would a tool that can convert emails into tickets to allow easier tracking of requests

Next, we need to be able to record information about the DSAR and the requesting data subject. This is required so we can start the internal process of finding all the relevant material. We also need the ability to attach documents to the ticket. These documents could be identification documents, or they could be information the data subject has provided.

A case management system needs to be able to assign and track tasks. Bear in mind the person who is coordinating all the activity relating to the DSAR is not going to be able to complete every part of it themselves. The DSAR coordinator will need to rely heavily on other people to support the process. Knowing where everybody is when you've got hundreds of requests coming in, and you're searching through potentially tens, hundreds, maybe even thousands of different databases and different systems, will require tracking.

You need to be able to have a very simple way of communicating with the data subject. As we mentioned earlier in the book DSARs can often originate from a botched complaint. It's therefore critical that you keep the data subject updated to prevent the issue escalating into a further complaint - this time to the regulator! For example, as the very first step you should acknowledge their request. In addition, you may need to ask the data subject for further information, or you may need to clarify the nature of the request. You may need to let them know that you are extending the timeframe in which you will reply and why this extension is necessary. We'll talk about the kind of responses you can provide to a data subject later in the book when we discuss communication, so don't panic if you think you have missed a chapter! In addition to communicating with the data subject you also need to be able to communicate with the relevant stakeholders within your organisation; within your third parties; and with your processors. You will need to keep a record of all communication between these parties and a case management tool that can track this is for you is essential should anything need following up.

And that leads on to the next 'must have' feature - the ability to track deadlines. In addition to communicating with relevant stakeholders it's crucial that you can track the deadlines you have assigned. If you've assigned a task to a stakeholder, or you've communicated with a third-party data processor, you really want a system that can remind you if that request hasn't received a response.

Your case management tool needs the ability to produce reports. Producing reports will help you to understand what your DSAR volumes are, how long it's taking to fulfil DSARs, and whether there are bottlenecks in your organisation's processes. It's useful to track other items too, for example, what are the issues that are causing DSARs? How many times have you applied a particular exemption? These, and other questions we will highlight in future chapters will, if you track them, help to create an efficient DSAR process.

You also need to make sure you have an audit trail. This is particularly important, for example, if someone makes a complaint against you to a Data Protection regulator because you've missed a deadline, or even because the data subject 'thinks' you've missed the deadline. Having the ability to go back to a data subject and say, "*Hey, this is when we received your request, here's all the evidence and here's what we've done.*" will go a long way in making sure that you keep the data subject on side.

Finally, and obviously, the case management system you use must be secure. Bear in mind as soon as you start processing DSARs in the case management system you're now processing personal data. The case management system in itself must be GDPR compliant. It may surprise some readers to learn you could already have a system you're using that will do all of these 'Must have' requirements. What is this system? It's your IT Help Desk or Service Desk system.

If you're not familiar with your organisation's Service Desk system its worth having a conversation with your IT Service Desk Manager. Try to establish the feasibility of using the service desk tool to process DSARs. The IT Service Desk Manager should be able to set you up with a licence to access the back end of the Service Desk Tool. They may also - if you ask nicely - provide you with some resources to help build forms and workflow to support your DSAR process. Whatever you decide to do, it is strongly recommended you investigate your organisation's Service Desk Tool before procuring any tool that focuses solely on DSAR case management. Whilst it may look like the easiest option to get a tool that works 'out of the box' such tools can become quite expensive. They may need additional hardware or have licencing costs, which would then limit how many people can access the tool. If your current Service Desk tool can do the job then save your limited budget for something more useful - like a Data Protection Analyst or two!

# File Encryption Tools

File encryption is the process of securing a file, or a collection of files, so only those with the secret key can access them. This can be particularly useful for those working on a DSAR where material is stored on a file system, that multiple people have access to, but not all need to know this particular information. File encryption can be used to securely transfer files where no other compatible mechanism exists between the sender and the recipient (e.g.. File encryption can also be used when sending electronic data on physical media where the chain of custody may be broken, or there is the possibility of the data becoming lost, for example in a postal system. An important distinction to make is that password protection of a file, as can be done with many desktop applications, does not necessarily mean the file is encrypted, or that the data cannot be accessed without the password. Some password protection mechanisms stop the casual user from accessing the data but won't stop a more determined antagonist!

When choosing a file encryption tool it's important to use a tool that is accessible to the data subject. The data subject should not have to pay to decrypt their data by having to buy a piece of software. The decryption mechanism – where possible - should work on the recipient's machine without the requirement for additional software and should also be simple to use. Some encrypted files can talk back to a control server to perform validation checks, and if such systems are used, it's important to ensure the recipient's security controls don't block these call-backs. Another factor to consider is the level of encryption possible. Be sure to check the encryption algorithm is currently secure. Over time, as computer power and security research develop, older algorithms once deemed secure can be easily compromised.

# File Hashing Tools

When initially collecting DSAR material it is useful to store a version of the data that does not get processed - a "clean" copy. Keeping a clean copy is worthwhile in the event data in a "working" copy is compromised. For example, data could be accidentally removed, or an exemption could be incorrectly applied, meaning you can no longer remove the one-way redaction. Having a clean copy can also save time should some, or all, of the processed data become corrupted. Should the worst case happen, and you need to legally defend your process, having a clean copy could be critical in demonstrating the DSAR process was followed correctly.

Unfortunately, with enough time and the right resources file-based encryption can be overcome, especially if the sender has used a weak password. You will need a way to confirm the file has not been tampered with in transit and where possible send encrypted files through secure channels where the chain of custody can be assured.

As the above examples highlight there are benefits to having verifiable copies of the DSAR material, both before processing, and when sending material over uncontrolled channels. So how can organisations ensure these "clean" copies have not been corrupted along the way? How can organisations ensure data has not been removed or content has not been modified? The answer to this is cryptographic hashing!

Whilst most people think of cryptography as a means of encrypting and decrypting files, cryptography can also be used to give data a unique digital fingerprint. This can be done at the sub-file level (e.g. fingerprinting a part of an image to prevent copyright violations or identify illegal content), at the file level (e.g. to confirm a single file has not been altered) or at a multi-file level (e.g. to validate that an entire corpus of data has not been altered). This technique, typically shortened to "hashing", involves running your file, of files, through a cryptographic hashing algorithm (e.g. MD5 or SHA512). By then keeping a record of the resulting hash value and making it known to the other party they can also check the value independently. There are many free hashing programmes out there. Examples include HashCheck, HashMyFiles and, if you're familiar with Windows PowerShell, you can also use the hashing tool built into the Windows OS called Get-Filehash. We'll be discussing hashing in more detail in Chapter Six.


## e-Discovery / Search

As we briefly touched upon earlier in the book - and will discuss further in later chapters - the built-in search facilities of your systems will be heavily relied upon to collect personal data. If you process personal data across multiple systems that initial data collection may need further processing to reduce the effort in later activities. Examples may include deduplication of data or removal of information incorrectly collected, e.g. due to limitations in the original system's search capabilities. If you're dealing with DSARs where you have collected hundreds of thousands of records, in many different file types and derived from several different systems, then you will most likely benefit from a separate e-discovery tool.

An e-discovery tool will aid the practitioner tasked with processing DSARs in several ways throughout the RAFM, and good e-Discovery tools will have case management functionality too. Case management functionality is typically baked into most commercial e-Discovery offerings. The case management described here, however, is separate from the wider case management described earlier in this section, and solely refers to keeping track of all your different search queries for a particular dataset. e-Discovery tools can also convert paper documents into electronic formats with the added benefit of performing optical character recognition (OCR) on the content. If you have a significant volume of a data subject's records in paper form, having this capability will be a saviour when it comes to activities such as identifying third parties, applying exemptions, and performing redaction. e-Discovery tools can also search through archives and compressed files (e.g. *.Zip, *.Rar) to find data that may not be feasible  using limited operating system search facilities. In terms of searches, e-

Discovery tools can be a lifesaver for systems where search functionality is limited or even non-existent. For example, if a system can be searched by a data subject's name, but not by date or linked identifiers, an e-Discovery tool could ingest a larger dataset and be used to narrow down the relevant results. Let us also consider searching through thousands of physical documents, in this instance such a tool would materially speed up what would otherwise be a horrendous manual process!

## Redaction Tools

In many cases the personal data of the requestor may be combined with the personal data of third parties. Such data, where it is not appropriate to provide it to the data subject, must be removed. There will also be scenarios where personal data related to the data subject is subject to an exemption and this takes priority over the right to access. Where an exemption applies the personal data and associated content must be removed and we will discuss this further in a later chapter.

So how is this achieved? The simplest way to remove exempted or third-party personal data would be to delete the entire file. However, this is not always feasible when the personal data in scope is in a contiguous form with other out-of-scope personal data, e.g. combined in an email or part email and part attachment. Where wholesale deletion could be described as using a chainsaw, what is often required is a more surgical approach to removing personal data...and for this, redaction is our scalpel!

Redaction is the process of obscuring text and rendering it unreadable. The "old school" approach to redaction is to print everything out and manually go through each page with a big fat marker pen, physically redacting any content deemed to be exempted. For those who have not been through such an exercise, we are sure you can already appreciate how time-consuming this can be. The amount of personal data generated by a single data subject in a short period – particularly if not applying data protection by design principles - can be substantial. In such a manual process a data protection professional will be faced with the prospect of reading thousands of sheets of paper and redacting each and every page by hand. They would then need to read through all that material again to check their work...surely there must be a better way?

Enter redaction software! Redaction software automates the process of removing personal data, or exempted material, from your initial DSAR. Good redaction software will typically have some, or all, of the following features.

Optical Character Recognition (OCR) is a means by which scanned physical documents can be read by software to identify text in the image. This text can then be searched. If you have a lot of physical documents, then OCR will be hugely beneficial. Simply scan all your documents and the OCR will find all the text contained on all the pages When OCR has created a digital, searchable, version of your document you can then also semi-automate redaction of any relevant material. This is because a lot of redaction software has the facility to "search once, redact all." This means when you have found a piece of personal data you wish to redact, you can then apply that redaction to the entire document – but you need the document in a searchable form first! A word of caution when using such features, most tools that can apply multiple redactions are unlikely to have the context to determine when to redact and when not to redact. This activity will, for the near future at least, still require human input. Another feature of good redaction software is the ability to apply redaction to wordlists, or phrase lists. Such features can significantly speed up the redaction process for standard document layouts. Let's say, for example, you are fulfilling a DSAR for a customer and need to redact all internal employee communication about that customer. A wordlist of employees could be used to apply mass redaction to all such internal emails.

## Secure Communication

At various points during the DSAR process there will be a requirement to communicate with the data subject. At the outset there may be a need to collect personal data to support the identification of the data subject. There may be a need to clarify the DSAR scope and there will eventually be a need to send the DSAR material. There may be a requirement to answer follow-up questions relating to the DSAR and all this communication must be secure. As part of setting up a DSAR processing environment, organisations need to consider how they will securely communicate with data subjects. It may be that organisations need to rely on more than one secure communication method too. For example, many personal email accounts have attachment file size limits, so if a DSAR involves gigabytes of data the sheer size of the files will mean it's not possible to send this material through email. Organisations cannot force data subjects to install tools on their computers to facilitate secure communications. Equally, organisations cannot force data subjects to make configuration changes (e.g. to enforce TLS) in the same way they may do when establishing a regular Business-to-Business (B2B) communication link. Organisations must provide secure communication with little impact on the data subject, and this doesn't leave many options!

So, what can organisations do? A useful exercise is to break down your communication needs based on the volume of data held. Where the volume of data is high, explore setting up a data room or portal, where data subjects can access their data and then download it themselves. Bear in mind, whether developing a portal in-house or procuring a third-party system, the system must be secure. It is vital you conduct appropriate security due diligence before exposing large volumes of personal data to the internet!

If portals, or data rooms, are not viable consider the use of physical media, but it is important to bear in mind whether the end-user will be able to access the material. Organisations sending data by CD/DVD/Blu-Ray may find the users' devices no longer have such drives fitted as standard. A USB flash drive is likely to be the most widely compatible option. Another consideration when it comes to physical media is to ensure material stored on the drive can only be accessed by the intended data subject. This is where the file encryption and file hashing discussed earlier will come in handy.

## Secure Storage

When good organisations build systems to store personal data, they will usually consider several controls.  They will spend tens of thousands of pounds on implementing security controls to lock down that system and keep the personal data safe. They will store the data in encrypted databases and monitor user activity for signs of compromise. They will implement backup and recovery systems and test, and re-test, to confirm these systems operate effectively. However, once a data protection practitioner extracts personal data to support a subject access request, all those controls are now redundant. It is now the responsibility of the data protection practitioner to ensure personal data is stored securely throughout the DSAR process. Therefore, when implementing a DSAR processing environment practitioners need to ensure they have a location to securely store personal data – but what does that mean? To securely store data, consider the following controls.

- Ensure there is a mechanism to provide access at an individual level. There should be no shared access and each user must have their own individual credentials.
- The interaction between the user and the personal data must be auditable. If a file is created, read, updated, or deleted (CRUD) then a log should be made of that action.
- There should be logs of any activity related to transferring data out of the secure storage area.
- The secure storage should come under the scope of the organisation's anti-malware controls and should have controls to prevent data leakage.
- The secure storage should be capable of implementing encryption at rest in a fault-tolerant way.

We know what encryption is but what is meant by "fault-tolerant"? Let's look at a real-life example. An organisation could process DSAR material on the hard drive of a laptop or desktop PC, and whilst encryption at rest is implemented on these personal devices, the possibility of unrecoverable hardware failure is high, and halfway through processing the laptop fails. In such hardware failure scenarios recovery of encrypted data is nigh on impossible. Instead of using the hard drive within a laptop or desktop, practitioners must use a network file share that is set up to protect against hardware failure. Technologies such as Redundant Array of Independent Disks (RAID) which can mirror data over more than one hard drive should be used. Cloud storage is typically set up to provide such redundancy and often provides encryption at rest by default – however, be sure to conduct your due diligence first before uploading anything to a third party's infrastructure!

# Secure Destruction

Many of you will already know when you delete something it is not necessarily fully deleted and deleting something to the extent it is unrecoverable can be challenging. The typical deletion process starts with the conscious act of pressing delete. From here the file, or files, go into the recycle bin – from where they can be recovered just in case you didn't mean to press delete! If you empty the recycle bin all that happens is an entry pointing to the physical location on the disk is obscured. Even when you remove that entry completely the file data can still be recovered. To securely destroy the data entirely you must overwrite the data itself.

For most cases in the commercial sector one pass of pseudorandom data over the original file will be sufficient to render the data unreadable. Where organisations may be processing particularly sensitive information they may wish, or be required, to overwrite the data using three overwrite passes. The first with all 1's, the second with all 0's and the third pass using pseudorandom data. You may hear people suggesting that unless you wipe the data thirty-five times there is still a chance it can be recovered. Technically, this may be true, but unless you own a pretty powerful electron microscope one to three passes will suffice.

Now, most modern operating systems (at the time of print) don't provide secure deletion out of the box. Additionally, you may be using cloud storage where overwriting tools will not function. So, what can you do to have comfort your files will not be retrievable post deletion? What options are available to securely delete data in these two common scenarios? There are two practical approaches. Where the data is stored on hard drives you control, third-party tools can be sourced from the Internet, and can securely delete data by conducting the one to three pass overwriting approach described earlier. Where the data is stored in the cloud, or storage you don't control, the files should be encrypted first with a strong 15-character complex password and then deleted.

Finally, when it comes to secure deletion, don't forget your backups and archives. If you have deleted files because you no longer need them ensure your IT department have processes in place to securely destroy the backup copies too.


# Knowledgebase / Wiki

Whilst this book will (hopefully) be useful in aiding you as you navigate the complexities of the DSAR process, you are still going to need to build your own organisation-specific policies, processes, procedures, and guidelines. Whilst it may be tempting to create stand-alone Word or PDF documents, a better approach is to use a Knowledgebase tool.

Knowledgebases are used commonly by IT departments for documenting how to deal with frequently occurring issues. They are used to document workarounds should someone have a problem with a particular system. They can also be used to support the provision of guidance on issues commonly experienced by a userbase.

Knowledgebases allow you to keep all your processes and procedures together, in one place, as a selection of knowledge articles. Articles don't always have to be written step-by-step guides; they could also be video tutorials. Best of all, articles can be shared with everyone in the organisation without having to give access to your department's folder system. Let's say you are constantly asked the same questions about what exemptions can be applied in a particular situation. The first time you are asked the question you can put the answer in the knowledge base. The next time someone asks, you can simply search for your previous answer, copy, and paste the response and you have saved yourself a lot of time. Better still, you could provide a link to the answer in a Frequently Asked Questions (FAQ) article.

A knowledge base will be an invaluable time-saving tool. It will be an essential training tool for your team and your colleagues in the wider organisation. Make sure you assign time to add to your knowledge base and make sure you keep the material under regular review as regulatory guidance changes.

## Mass Document Scanner

Whilst many organisations have become pretty much paperless, some are still heaped in reams upon reams of physical documents. These documents are often in indexed boxes stored in a warehouse or backroom. Physical documents containing personal data[5] still fall within the scope of a Data Subject Access Request. They must be reviewed and redacted where appropriate. Making copies and doing all the DSAR work by hand when there are thousands of pieces of paper involved is going to be a severe drain of resources – a soul-destroying task!

A mass document scanner does exactly what it says on the tin. Thousands of sheets of paper can be fed through the scanner at pace. Optical Character Recognition (OCR) can be applied to the electronic versions of the paper documents and the documents are then searchable. The ability to search through the document set will substantially reduce the review and redaction process. If reviewing thousands of physical documents is something you are likely to deal with frequently, investment in a mass document scanner is going to be invaluable!

---

[5] When stored in a relevant filing system.

## Audio / Video Editor

When processing DSARs that involve the output of systems such as call recording software or CCTV you will need a way to review and edit video and audio files. The solution we recommend is to process these files through off-the-shelf video editing software that can apply visual effects and masks using keyframes or object tracking. There are several free and paid options that have these features - DaVinci Resolve and Hit Film are free at time of print and Adobe Premier, which is paid for, can all perform these tasks. But what are object tracking and keyframes and why are they important? At a very basic level these features allow the user to blur certain parts of an image, e.g., a third party's face, over multiple frames of video. Without this capability the footage would need to be blurred frame by frame which could take weeks!

So, there you have it, a DSAR shopping list of tools! As mentioned at the beginning of this section not all these tools are required. But, if you're finding yourself overwhelmed in one or more areas, these tools will make your life easier. Don't rush into getting all these tools at once though. Firstly, review your organisation's DSAR demand, review the effort needed to keep on top of things and then consider whether one, or more, of the tools suggested could improve efficiency AND efficacy.

So, now we know what tools we may need, let's move onto training!

# Train

It should be obvious, but we'll say it anyway…training is essential! It's not just training for yourself and it's not just training for your team. In order to get DSARs right, there must be training in place to cover your whole organisation. In this section, we will discuss the training that is required in most organisations to ensure DSARs are fulfilled in a manner compliant with the major data protection regulations across the world.

First up, determining your training needs…

## Are you ready to be a Trainer?

Now, training is not something that everyone is born to do. Training is not simply putting a slide deck together, standing at the front of a meeting room and talking confidently for 35-40mins. Training requires preparation. This book is not a guide to providing corporate training, but we do want to steer you towards good practice. If you are going to deliver training we strongly recommend finding an Education and Training course in your local area. These courses will give you the knowledge and help to develop your skills as a trainer in any subject you know enough about. A good course will assess your teaching ability in the form of a practice lesson that you will be required to plan and deliver. At time of print, courses cost around £250-500 for an entry level qualification in the UK.

## The Training Programme

Whether you will be delivering training personally, or you get someone else in, your organisation will need a training programme. Whether you look at the right to access as a discrete issue, or as part of a wider data protection agenda, one of the first activities you should do is develop your training programme. A training programme, at its heart, will consist of the following components that take you from identifying your desired business outcomes, to creating and delivering training, and then assessing its effectiveness. Let's look at each in more detail:

**Identify desired business outcomes**: Document the behavioural change you wish to achieve and give each learning objective a unique identifier for tracking. The more specific your business outcomes the better. Ensure you conduct a baseline assessment against each outcome before you start the training programme. This will allow you to determine the effectiveness of the training when it has been completed.

Some examples of learning outcomes could be:

- o **[DSAR-LO-001]** Improve identification of DSARs across the business. Zero DSARs missed by CSRs.
- o **[DSAR-LO-002]** Reduce the time taken to search information systems for relevant personal data by 10%
- o **[DSAR-LO-003]** Reduce the time taken for the DPO to be informed of DSARs by 2 days from current average.
- o **[DSAR-LO-004]** Reduce the amount of personal data stored past retention deadline to zero outside litigation hold.
- o **[DSAR-LO-005]** Reduce the number of complaints relating to incorrect exemptions applied to DSARs to zero.
- o **...and so on...**

**Link learning outcomes to organisational roles**: Which roles need behavioural change? Consider that behavioural change may be required in multiple roles to achieve the desired outcomes. Consider the priority for training each role (0 = No Priority, 5 = High Priority). Taking the examples above we could produce the following table:

| Role: | Customer Service Reps | Head of IT | System Business Owner | DPO | Role X |
|---|---|---|---|---|---|
| **Outcome:** | | | | | |
| **DSAR-LO-001** | 5 | 2 | 2 | 5 | ? |
| **DSAR-LO-002** | 0 | 4 | 5 | 5 | ? |
| **DSAR-LO-003** | 5 | 1 | 1 | 5 | ? |
| **DSAR-LO-004** | 0 | 4 | 5 | 5 | ? |
| **DSAR-LO-005** | 0 | 0 | 0 | 5 | ? |
| **DSAR-LO-XXX** | ? | ? | ? | ? | ? |

*Figure 7 - Learning Outcomes by Role*

**Create training objectives for each organisational role**: After training priorities are identified it is then time to create Training Objectives for each role. Training Objectives should clearly articulate the knowledge, skills and behaviours required for a particular role. For example, in the table above, it has been identified there is a high priority training requirement for Customer Service Representatives (CSRs). Specifically in relation to identifying DSARs and a need to quickly communicate any DSARs to their Data Protection Officer. These prioritised learning outcomes can now be translated into the following Training Objectives:

- o **[CSR-TO-DSAR-001]** Understand that a data subject can make a Data Subject Access Request via any of our current customer channels (e.g. Email, Phone, Social-Media) - *Knowledge*
- o **[CSR-TO-DSAR-002]** Recognise a Data Subject Access Request even when the request does not explicitly refer to data protection or subject access requests – *Knowledge + Skill*
- o **[CSR-TO-DSAR-003]** Know the procedure to be followed when a customer makes a DSAR – *Knowledge*
- o **[CSR-TO-DSAR-004]** – Communicates all suspected DSARs to the Data Protection within 2 hours of receipt. *Skill + Behaviour*
- o **...and so on...**

An effective way to validate whether you have created successful training objectives is to determine how the objective will be assessed. There are many different ways to assess knowledge, skill, and behaviours and some common assessment methods are scenario-based questions, desk-based "walk-through-talk-through" assessments, and the use of mystery shoppers. The key is to make sure you use an appropriate method for each objective. Scenario-based questions are great for knowledge, but not so much for skills and behaviours, where a practical assessment would be more appropriate.

**Identify training resources**: OK, you have identified your outcomes and ascertained who needs to be trained. Now you need to identify who is going to be conducting the training and, equally as important, how they are going to conduct the training. As we mentioned earlier, just because you are a Data Protection Officer, or an expert in how to navigate the Data Subject Access Request process, unfortunately does not automatically make you a competent trainer. Even if you are a half-decent trainer, you still may not be able to deliver all the required training. For example, you may work in an organisation with tens of 1000s of employees, and you simply don't have the time to deliver all the required training. You may work in a multinational organisation and don't speak every language spoken. Sure, you may find that the Head Office teams in each country may speak a single international language but those working in the Customer Service Centres may only speak their local language.

It's not just about your limitations to deliver either, you need to also consider whether everyone can receive the training in the medium you provide it. Thus, you need to consider your organisational structure and the equipment available to each employee. Some DPOs seem to think they can clone themselves by creating computer based training (CBT) and then sending out an email missive with a deadline...but forget that many of their employees don't have access to laptops or computers because their roles don't require such equipment. The timing of training is also important, especially when people work shifts. Likewise, accessibility must be considered for employees who have specific needs, for example, some employees may need to make use of a screen reader or other assistive technology.

Now, we have mentioned computer-based training as an option to expand your reach, but it must not be the only option! CBT is not going to be an appropriate training tool for many of the knowledge, skills, and behaviours you will be trying to embed across your organisation. For example, it is highly unlikely that CBT could be used to train system administrators how to conduct reasonable searches of a database. CBT is equally unlikely to be an appropriate method to train employees how to redact documents.

If you are delegating the training to others, make sure you organise preview sessions to verify the quality and relevance of training. This is especially important when outsourcing training to a contractor or third-party provider. Remember external sources don't necessarily know how your specific business operates, so try to find a training provider who at the very least has sector specific training material.

Essentially, identify and procure resources that best suit your employees' training needs and make it real for them. **Whatever you do, don't be that person who thinks because it works for you, it'll work for everyone!**

**Implement Training**: This is the penultimate step in your training programme. It's time to get out there and deliver the package of training. Be sure to keep marketing training sessions throughout the delivery phase to ensure maximum participation. Make sure you keep records of those who have attended sessions and follow up with those who have yet to complete their training. People will sometimes be called out to deal with emergencies or other situations so it's important to have the flexibility that allows people to re-attend where necessary.

Remember to make your sessions as interactive as possible. Workplace training should be a two-way educational process where you as the trainer also learn from your "students". Pay attention to the questions asked and the operational practices participants discuss. Take note of statements such as "that won't work in my area" and find out why. Listen out for discussions on ancillary issues, that may not necessarily be relevant to the Right of Access, but instead highlight other data protection issues that need to be addressed.

**Assess effectiveness**: The final step is to establish how well the training improved the knowledge, skills, and behaviours of your employees. Remember in step one you conducted a pre-training baseline assessment of your employee's knowledge, skills, and behaviours? Hopefully! Well, now it's time to conduct a post-training assessment. Are your desired business outcomes being met? If not, identify the issues and modify your training programme accordingly. If the business outcomes are being met, that's great.. Remember, though, that training can lose its effectiveness over time so be sure to keep assessing effectiveness periodically to make sure standards don't drop!

# Summary

The primary focus of this chapter was to review the preparation phase of the Right of Access Fulfilment Model. The preparation phase has two sub-components – resource and train. Both components will give you a solid foundation from which to build an effective and efficient Data Subject Access Request programme.

We initially reviewed the resources required for your DSAR programme, noting that not all resources will be needed for all programmes, and some resources will only be required in organisations dealing with significant volumes or cases with high levels of complexity. It was highlighted that good case management software will make life easier. However, that does not necessarily mean there is a need to buy data protection specific case management software. A Customer Service tool or an IT service desk should be more than suitable in most organisations with a little bit of customisation.

We then discussed training. Training for yourself as a Data Protection lead and training for all employees. As mentioned way back at the beginning of this book, a significant proportion of complaints to the UK Data Protection Regulator (ICO) are right to access related. This metric highlights that organisations are not getting DSARs right and suggests training in many organisations is not adequate. It's therefore incumbent upon you, as the person leading your programme, to ensure there is appropriate investment in organisation-wide training. Even if you're not the one delivering it, training is essential.

Whilst we have discussed preparation in this phase, a key component of preparation is to fully understand all the stages of the RAFM in detail. With that in mind, let's keep our momentum going and look at the first operational stage of the RAFM – Collection.

# Chapter Six - Collection Phase

*Figure 8 - Collection Phase*

As initially discussed in chapter three, the collection phase aims to collect the material requested of a data subject in the most efficient manner possible, and getting the collection phase wrong can substantially increase your workload.

The three sub-components of the RAFM collection phase are **Verify, Search** and **Preserve**. In the verify section we will look at how to confirm the identity of the data subject and how to lock down exactly what it is they are looking to access. We will touch on some specific types of data, e.g., education, employment, and health. Finally, we will wrap up the section by discussing time limits.

In the search section we will look at how to plan and conduct searches for personal data. We will then work through the creation of an identification plan. We will look at how to document collection instructions so those who own the databases know exactly what to search for. We will look at different search techniques to help those searching find the correct information and then wrap up with a brief discussion on inferred Personal Data.

In the Preserve section we will look at techniques to preserve personal data records. First, we will discuss a concept called litigation hold. This deals with preserving data so it isn't automatically get deleted at the end of a pre-determined retention period. We will then discuss how to preserve a clean copy of the DSAR prior to the Treatment phase.

Let's get cracking!

# Verify

Verification is the first step in the Collection process. Getting verification right will significantly reduce the amount of material that will be treated in later parts of the DSAR process and avoid inadvertent security breaches (e.g., the Personal Data of one data subject being provided to another data subject in error). In this section we will cover the steps a controller should incorporate into their processes to make sure they have: -

- a valid request from a legitimate source
- identified the correct data subject so as to support internal search processes.
- a confirmed and clear scope as to what material the data subject requires.
- a clear deadline for when the DSAR must be fulfilled.

## Verifying Reasonable Adjustments

In certain cases, a data subject may have a disability that prevents them from either making a subject access request in a specific way or receiving the data in a specific medium – or perhaps both. In these scenarios, the controller should (and in some cases may be compelled by local legislation) to make reasonable adjustments to their standard DSAR process to support the data subject.

Thus, the first step verification phase is to understand whether any reasonable adjustments need to be made. When considering making reasonable adjustments a controller will need to understand what their local equalities or disabilities legislation requires. This local legislation should tell you whether your type of organisation falls within its scope and will also set out any minimum requirements. Additionally, your organisation may also have a policy related to reasonable adjustments so you should check the requirements detailed in this document too. If you're not sure whether your organisation has such a document, it's worth contacting your HR department as reasonable adjustments is likely to form part of your organisation's HR processes. Once you understand what is required, you should then create an action plan of items to implement within your DSAR process. If you don't have specific legislation or policy that covers reasonable adjustments, it's still a very good idea to make reasonable adjustments anyway! Let's have a look at some examples that you may wish to consider when developing a DSAR process.

- Ensuring those with disabilities can make a DSAR. E,g. A customer service representative taking down a request over the phone instead of fobbing the data subject off to send the request by email to another department.
- Incorporating telephone/videoconference methods and templates into your processes e.g., carrying out identity checks over the telephone instead of via email.
- Providing the DSAR material large print format or using braille.

- If in electronic form, ensuring the DSAR material is fully compatible with screen reading technology.
- Ensuring DSARs are not automatically deemed manifestly excessive or unfounded. For example, someone who uses profane language may be suffering from a medical condition such as Tourette's. Another person may have learning difficulties and may not be able to properly form a coherent request.
- Training your staff to be aware of the reasonable adjustments and the need to provide appropriate support to those with disabilities.

This list is not exhaustive and only serves to give you some things to consider. The key thing is that data subjects with disabilities, whether physical or mental in nature, still have the right to access their personal data in a way that means they can read and interact with material.

# Verifying the Data Subject

If you're lucky DSARs may just contain a small amount of personal data in the form of a few database entries and perhaps a handful of emails. In reality DSARs are likely to contain a lot of personal data, including special category data, and potentially thousands of pieces of correspondence across multiple messaging systems. The material in the DSAR is likely to be sensitive to the data subject and may have legal ramifications for the controller. It is therefore essential the controller verifies the material they search for, and find, across their systems is the personal data of the data subject making the request. It is entirely possible that your databases hold records for two (or more) separate individuals with exactly the same name. So, before any searches are carried out, a controller needs to make sure the correct data subject is identified.

Verifying the identity of the data subject may not always be straightforward. To make matters worse systems are not always set up with fool proof ways of uniquely identifying one individual from another without additional contextual information. When initialising a DSAR consider your exposure to such a situation and collect contextual information from the data subject accordingly. For example, if the data subject has been an employee ask them to provide their National Insurance / Social Security number to uniquely identify the requestor. Alternatively, if you routinely collect personal data, other than that which has been provided in the request, e.g., Date of Birth, Address or Telephone Number, ask for this information to be provided. Collection of such contextual information could also form part of your identification checks and there will be more on this in the next section. What a controller should avoid doing is collecting additional personal data unless absolutely necessary.

# Checking Identification

In addition to confirming the identity of the data subject for the purposes of collecting the right material, it is also important to verify the person making the DSAR is actually who they say they are. An abuser could, for example, fake a DSAR to find out the location of their victim. A deranged fan could fake a DSAR to gain insights into the private life of their favourite celebrity. A controller must ensure DSAR material is protected from scenarios where a person could be trying to obtain the material of someone else fraudulently.

A controller's identity check must be sufficient to verify the person is who they say they are, whilst at the same time collecting the absolute minimum in additional personal data. The check must actually use the personal data that has been collected. For example, asking a person to send in a copy of their passport or driving licence when a controller has no way to verify whether the document is genuine would not be appropriate. Similarly, asking for a utility bill, or other random document, just because it has their personal data on it is equally unsuitable. If however, you already have a copy of a passport to verify the copy sent by the requestor, this would be more appropriate – unless a less intrusive mechanism was available. controllers must also be mindful that if someone has fraudulently managed to gain access to a data subject's legitimate email they may have access to identity documents the data subject already has stored in their mailbox. It is therefore much better to ask questions of the data subject that relate to their use of your services which are not manifestly made public. For example, if you are an eCommerce site, ask the data subject to name the last thing they purchased from you. Perhaps get your software development team to create a feature on your app/website where the user must log in and enter a 6-digit code sent to their mobile device to verify their identity. The main consideration is to be proportionate, whilst at the same time minimising any additional risk that an excessive identity check process could accidentally cause, e.g., if that additional data was exfiltrated by hackers during a cyber security incident.

A word of warning with regards to identity checks. Practitioners can sometimes become so focused on demonstrating an identity check has been conducted, that they neglect the steps to check they have the correct data subject. As a result they still end up giving the material related to one data subject to someone else who happens to share the same name. Make sure you incorporate both verifying you have the correct data subject, AND that the requestor is who they say they are, into your organisation's verification checklist.

# Verifying the right to access made by a Third Party

There may be cases where a third party is acting on behalf of a data subject. This could be a parent/guardian (in the case of their children), or perhaps a solicitor on behalf of a client. Other third parties may also attempt to make a DSAR purporting to have the authority of the data subject in question, such as an insurance provider, the courts, or a spouse. In all cases where a third party is relying on the right to access granted to a data subject as the basis for their request, the controller must ensure they have sufficient comfort the request is valid and, where appropriate, authorised by the data subject. This could involve contacting the data subject to gain their permission or it could be to see notarised copies of an applicable authority to act on behalf of the data subject (e.g., a Power of Attorney or equivalent). Where it is not appropriate to contact the data subject directly, the data subject does not provide consent, or does not reply within a reasonable period of time, then the DSAR should not be fulfilled.

# Verifying the Request

When you know you're dealing with the correct data subject, or an authorised third party, the next thing you should consider verifying is the nature of the request itself. A controller should communicate with the data subject as early as possible to ask whether they are looking for something specific or for something within a specified date range. In doing so the controller may be able to narrow the scope of the DSAR to only include the information the data subject would like. In many cases, if the relationship has not completely soured, the data subject will usually be happy to let you know the specific data they want to access. For example, a data subject may believe records held by the controller are incorrect and may wish to get a copy, highlight the inaccuracies, and then exercise their right to rectification. When a controller seeks to narrow the scope the outcome should then be mutually beneficial - the data subject will get their data more quickly and the controller will have less work to do to process the request. A controller must, however, be mindful that the data subject does not have to narrow the scope of their DSAR. If they want everything you have, and if it's not covered by an exemption, that's what the controller needs to provide.

Notwithstanding narrowing the scope, a DSAR may not actually be a DSAR in the first place. The person making the request may be asking for information that is covered by sectoral or national legislation. You may be able to save yourself a massive amount of work if you can clarify whether the data subject is making the request under sectoral or national rules, or they are relying on GDPR specifically. By way of example in the following sub-sections we will discuss some of the issues related to education, employment, and health data.

## Right to Access or Freedom of Information

Under many data protection regimes there are two common ways information can be obtained from an organisation. One way is through a data subject's right to access and this relates solely to accessing their personal data. Another way is through a freedom of information request. The latter typically does not cover access to personal data and is more concerned with facilitating transparency in public sector bodies i.e. so the electorate knows all that taxation is being prudently spent on effective public services. The thing is data subjects generally aren't expert data protection lawyers and often mix up these pieces of legislation. It is not uncommon for a data subject to say they want to make a freedom of information request when they actually want to make a DSAR instead. As a controller who falls under the scope of freedom of information legislation you may not necessarily employ the same people to deal with both freedom of information requestions and DSARs. It's therefore important to consider how DSARs incorrectly referencing freedom of information legislation are passed to the right team. Remember, a person making a DSAR does not have to state the correct legislation for the request to be valid so it's important to have a process to handle such situations.

## Right to Access to Education Data

In educational settings DSARs are often made by parents on behalf of their child. It is therefore important to be mindful that, in most cases, a child is a data subject themselves and has the same right to prevent another person (i.e., their parents/guardians) accessing personal data held about them by a controller. There are two main exceptions. The first is where the child is not deemed competent to exercise their own rights. In a situation where the child is not deemed competent a parent can make a DSAR on their child's behalf. It is important to ensure the child is not being compelled to make a DSAR when they don't wish to do so, however, determining whether this is the case could be challenging. For a start, there is no universal age in which a child is deemed competent. Any age codified will vary from jurisdiction to jurisdiction, and even with a codified age, there are other factors, i.e., a medical condition that may affect an older child's ability to competently exercise their rights. If you are unsure you should discuss the matter with your DPO who will be able to advise you in more detail about your specific case.

The second exception is where other legislation applies that grants a third-party access to your data without your express consent. For example, even where a data subject is deemed competent, in many jurisdictions around the world those with parental responsibility have a legal right of access to certain educational data about their child. The data involved will be a subset of the data that would be provided in a DSAR and may be referred to as a Pupil Record or an Education Record. Where relevant legislation exists a parent would have the right to access their children's Pupil Record independently of any rights afforded directly to the child under data protection law.

An example of other legislation granting third-party access to data is the Education (Pupil Information) (England) Regulations 2005 in England.  This gives those with parental responsibility the right to access their child's education record from a school covered by the legislation. This legislation also imposes a stricter 15-day deadline to respond rather than the 30-day deadline for a DSAR. It is, therefore, essential those receiving requests from parents of data subjects understand which legislation applies to the request. Parents, not entirely sure of their rights, may mistakenly make requests for education data under data protection legislation when the Education (Pupil Information) (England) Regulations 2005 would actually be more appropriate. Education providers should be mindful of parents misunderstanding and should not refuse to provide education data that parents are legally entitled to simply because the parent has referenced incorrect legislation. Instead, when responding to such requests, education providers should explain to parents what education data they are entitled to access directly. Education providers should also be mindful of any shorter deadlines and not process a request for education records as a DSAR in an attempt to gain extra time!

## Right to Access to Employment Data

In a similar way to personal data related to education there are nuances related to employment data that should be considered. Several data protection regulators, including the UK ICO, have provided guidance specifically related to dealing with DSARS that include employment data. There are some documents that are either provided by a data subject, or created during the employment process, that may not have personal data within the document directly, but it would be easy to reidentify an individual using the content of the material. As a result the material must be included in the DSAR unless it is covered by an appropriate exemption.

For example, during recruitment a HR team may choose to anonymise CVs by transferring the CV material into a standard template without identifiers, e.g., name, email, phone number etc, but to keep track of the application process a unique identifier is included in the document. At some point a hiring manager decides to interview a candidate and makes notes during the interview. They don't include any personal data but do include the same unique identifier included on the CV. The hiring manager produces a scoring matrix for all candidates interviewed and again includes the unique identifier. All this material falls within the scope of the Data Subject Access Request. Even if the unique identifier is only unique in the context of a specific role (and so one could argue anonymous in a wider context), the fact the CV material is included means a data subject could be easily identified from their unique work history alone across all the documents that contain the same identifier.

In contrast to being entitled to material that may at first look like it doesn't contain personal data, a data subject making a DSAR as an employee is not always entitled to a copy of every document when there is no doubt their personal data is present. For example, an employee may have their name in the to/cc/bcc fields of thousands of company emails. These emails will all therefore contain the personal data of the data subject, but even so, the data subject is not entitled to copies of all those emails, redacted or otherwise. We will talk more about how to deal with this, and similar situations, in more detail in Chapter Seven.

## Right to Access to Health Data

Continuing the theme there are also nuances in access to health data. In a similar way to education data, there will be situations where a parent may seek to access health information related to their child. As a general rule competency considerations equally apply when it comes to health care data in much the same way as they do for education related data. However, unlike education data health data will, in most cases, fall under the definition of special category data. Providing health data to the wrong person, even a parent, could potentially cause serious harm and distress.

There may be situations where a third party is attempting to support a person who has not been deemed competent under mental health legislation. There could be situations where a next of kin may be making a request for health records. The police or even insurance companies, are other examples of third parties who may request access to data. Some jurisdictions may allow disclosure to such third parties, however in other jurisdictions may compel the controller to rigorously enforce their duty of confidentiality. To avoid getting this catastrophically wrong ensure you take legal advice to determine which health-related legislation applies to subject access requests in the jurisdiction(s) within which you operate.

A further nuance to health-related data are requests for information about a person who has died. Many data protection laws, such as UK and EU GDPR, only cover living people. Organisations might be briefly forgiven for thinking the personal data of the deceased can therefore be provided to whomever makes a request. This is not the case in many jurisdictions. In the UK, for example, access to the health records of those who have died is covered by the Access to Health Care Records (AHR) Act (1990). This act allows personal representatives, for example, those tasked with executing the deceased's Last Will and Testament, and those who believe they have a claim arising from the deceased person's death, access to the deceased person's health records under certain circumstances. The AHR Act (1990) has different deadlines for fulfilling a request to those covered under UK data protection legislation. It's important to understand the deadlines that apply in your jurisdiction to be sure requests are fulfilled on time.

## Verifying Time Limits

Data Subject Access Requests typically have a legally mandated deadline for the controller to provide the requested material, however, as you have just seen there could be more than one relevant deadline. It is therefore essential practitioners verify which time limits apply to each request. In addition to the standard deadlines that apply some data protection legislation may permit the controller extra time should a request be particularly challenging to fulfil. In the UK/EU this can be up to an additional two months. Extensions are, however, only to be used in exceptional circumstances relating to the complexities of a specific DSAR. It's also worth repeating that extensions should not be used simply because a controller has too many DSARs running in parallel and adequate resources have not been made available. Those fulfilling DSARs should not pad the time out either. If it only takes two to three days to process the material, and even if you think the data subject is annoying, get the material to them as soon as possible. DSARs are usually linked to other issues which could potentially have life changing implications for the data subject. Getting the information to them quickly could mean any underlying issues can be cleared up and concluded quickly. When deadlines have been verified, and regardless of how long the DSAR will take to fulfil in practice, , the likely date the DSAR material will be provided should be communicated to the data subject as soon as possible.

Taking all of the above information into account let's look at a potential real-life example. A parent in the UK makes a DSAR to a controller who is an education provider. Initially, the controller considers the deadline for the request by applying the deadline stated in UK GDPR - 30 days. However, upon clarification of the request, a competent child refuses to allow the parent who made the original DSAR to act on their behalf. As a result of the child's refusal, the parent is only entitled to the child's education record. As this request then falls under the Education (Pupil Information) (England) Regulations 2005, and not UK GDPR, the deadline to provide the requested information is now 15 days. When the above is confirmed, the controller should inform the parent the information they are entitled to will be given on a date no later than 15 days from the request.

## Manifestly excessive or unfounded requests

Depending on the scope of your legislation, there may be circumstances where the nature of the data subject's request is deemed to be manifestly excessive or unfounded. In such situations a controller may be able to refuse to comply with the request. You must however be sure your justification is lawful. For example, refusing a request because you have retained thousands of emails relating to the data subject far past the period you need to would not be considered a lawful justification for refusing the request. Whatever the reason for considering a request to manifestly excessive or unfounded, a controller must communicate that the request will not be processed, the reason for not processing the request and that the data subject has the right to make a complaint to the relevant data protection regulator. An example of such a communication between a controller and data subject can be found in chapter 8.

# Search

Now we have verified the identity of the data subject, confirmed the details of the Data Subject Access Request, and agreed the time limits to provide the material, that's the easy bit done! Someone now needs to collect all the material that makes up the DSAR. Yes, that's right, all the data subject's personal data, and supporting material, needs to be collected from all the controller's systems and any systems managed by processors. Depending on how long the data subject has had a relationship with the organisation this could be a significant amount of material. We therefore need to be smart in the way we collect this information. Ensure you collect all the information needed to fulfil the request whilst minimising the collection of OPD – Other People's Data! As you may remember from the RAFM introduction in Chapter 3 when we have collected data we then need to treat it. So, the less unnecessary data we collect, the less unnecessary data we need to treat! This is why we need to be smart about our searching.

In this section, we are going to deep dive into how to conduct searches intelligently. Searching is not just a case of whacking the name of the data subject into a search engine and exporting the results. Taking such an approach could generate millions of potentially irrelevant records. Searching needs to be smart and planned! Planning your searches will ensure time and resources are not wasted in a) searching systems that don't hold data on a data subject and b) searching for data that isn't related to the specific data subject. A good search plan will also ensure you don't unintentionally send data about one data subject another different data subject – and all the consequent headaches that would result of such an error! Let's dive in!

## Relevant Filing Systems

In the introduction to this section, we briefly mentioned the term 'relevant filing system', but what makes a filing system 'relevant' to the DSAR process, and why is understanding this term important? It is essential to know whether a filing system is relevant or not as is if the file system is not 'relevant', then the data held within that 'nonrelevant' filing system falls out of scope of the DSAR process. The reverse is equally true. If the filing system is 'relevant' the data held is within scope of the DSAR. As we rely less and less on paper records and the search capabilities of our digital tools become more sophisticated the relevance of the relevant filing system term is diminishing. That said, there are still reasons why nonrelevant filing systems are used and this is primarily when creating manual paper-based records.

Now, before you set out on an organisation-wide policy of abandoning data structuring of manual records to avoid having to deal with DSARs anymore we would caution against it. It's highly likely that, whilst such a move may reduce the cost of DSARs, trying to then use this totally unstructured data to run your business will be considerably more costly! As we mentioned in reducing the DSAR burden section of chapter two, data minimisation is a much more effective strategy! So, what is a relevant filing system? Basically, it's a manual filing structure that allows 'ready access' e.g., through some form of organisation to information held on a specific data subject. Let's say a school creates a paper-based record for each of their students and has a process that requires the pupil records to be stored in a filing cabinet in alphabetical order. This would be a relevant filing system. Equally, if the same school places dividers for each letter of the alphabet and stores each pupil record within the relevant section that corresponded to the pupil's surname, this would also be a relevant filing system. The key thing to consider is how easy it is to find a particular record should it be needed for a business purpose. If a record can be readily accessed, then it's highly likely that the record is contained in a relevant filing system.

Now some readers may have noted the first example involved a process to store the data in a way that was directly linked to the individual. A relevant filing system could also exist if there is a process to access the data about an individual too. For example, the same school may hold performance reports about pupil progress. These reports are filed in separate places by subject. There is, however, a process to pull all the records together to provide an overall performance report for the pupil at the end of each year. Because there is a process to compile this personal data from each of the subject files this would also constitute a relevant filing system – even if it would take time and effort to pull it all together. Other commonly used approaches when organising data, such as using a person's name as the file name, or organising data by type of information (e.g., Leave requests) are also likely to be structured in such a way that they form part of a relevant filing system.

Having read the last paragraph, you may be asking yourself whether a non-relevant filing system could possibly exist? Well, there is at least one – notebooks. Where notes are contained in notebooks that contain personal data AND the data is not structured, such notebooks would not constitute a relevant filing system. That said, and there is often an exception, notebooks can form part of a relevant filing system in certain situations. For example, if you take interview notes as part of your hiring process and these notes are contained in a notebook marked "interviews", with each set of notes headed with the name of a candidate, or a unique identifier, with the date of the interview, this will then bring your notebook back into the scope of being a relevant filing system.

# The Identification Plan

OK, so we now understand that both paper and digital records are in the scope of a DSAR when they form part of a relevant filing system, we now need to go out and find all the material relating to the data subject in question. We therefore need a plan – an identification plan! The Identification Plan is exactly what it says on the tin. It's a means of planning how you are going to identify all the DSAR material you need to pull together. It helps you ensure you get the DSAR completed in the most efficient manner possible, and when you've got lots of things to do, that's always very helpful. Even in the simplest of DSARs an Identification Plan will ensure you think things through in a logical way. If, for example, after a DSAR is completed a complaint is made, the Identification Plan will be a really helpful tool in demonstrating to a Data Protection Regulator that you have made a reasonable effort to provide the information requested by the data subject. Hopefully, by pulling a plan together in the way we will describe you won't need to worry about that!

So, what is contained in the Identification Plan? To put it simply, the plan is an offshoot, or an operationalised version, of your Record of Processing Activity (RoPA). The ID plan takes filtered information from your RoPA and from that information you can assign data collection tasks to the right people. Before we go into detail about how we create an Identification Plan, and what should be in one, it's worth taking a minute to discuss a few things that help make identification easier. Knowing these will help you create a better plan - and a better plan should make the DSAR process run a lot more smoothly.

The key factors that make identification of personal data simpler and easier are as follows:

**Availability of a Record of Processing Activity and Data Maps**: As was mentioned previously you will need to filter a Record of Processing Activities. If you don't have a Record of Processing Activities already in place, then it's going to be a lot more challenging to filter your data. Similarly, if you don't have Data Maps then it's going to be tricky to look at how data flows from one system into another and where one process moves into another.

**Knowing Custodians, Keywords and Data Ranges**: These three components are helpful in identifying the data you are looking for and narrowing down where you're going to look for it. Knowing who runs the system and how that system is managed is going to be important. Knowing the keywords you're looking for is also going to be crucial in terms of ensuring all the relevant data is accounted for. The final component of keywords will be covered in a later section.

**Date Ranges**: Where a DSAR involves an employee, or ex-employee, of your organisation knowing when they joined, and potentially left the organisation, will help you narrow down your searches. Similarly, when someone became a customer or their relationship with your organisation changed, will also help in narrowing down the date range of data to be searched.

**Knowledge of Systems containing Personal Data:** This should speak for itself. If you know how these systems operate; how they store data; how to generate reports; and how to pull information from these systems, it is going to be helpful in ensuring your identification of personal data runs smoothly.

**Availability of Tools:** It should make sense that if you have the right tools to pull data, to search your systems, to communicate with the custodians and to track your DSARs these tools are going to make the process a whole lot simpler. We will look in more detail as to what these tools are in further sections.

**The Ability to Conduct Searches:** The ability to conduct searches is going to be a vital part of your armoury in conducting DSARs. Now, you may think you can conduct searches ... but there is searching, and then there is really searching! For example, you may need to use Boolean searches or wildcards, and we'll talk again about how to conduct searches in a separate section. If you don't have the ability to conduct searches and need to search manually, or you must create data dumps and filter in something like Excel, then this is going to make your life much more difficult.

**Exclusion Filters:** Conducting searches using personal data as identifiers can return results from automated sources. These results may not be relevant to the data subject's request. For example, a bank might send multiple automated reports to several thousand employees on a daily basis. These generic emails do contain personal data and so consequently fall within the scope of a DSAR. We will discuss treatment of these types of emails in more detail in chapters seven and eight and explain why they can be excluded. For now though, where generic emails don't need to be included in the DSAR, it is prudent to filter them out automatically as part of your search strategy. This is achieved by creating exclusion filters. Exclusion filtering will vary depending on the organisation but good candidates for exclusion filters are generic mailboxes such as "noreply@" or "reports@". In other situations, you could possibly exclude based on the "To" field of an email, e.g., "To: all-staff-distro".

A quick piece of advice when it comes to filtering on the subject line of emails. Many recipients may forward generic emails and add additional content that may be specific to a particular data subject. As a result, we do not recommend filtering based on subject line alone. If subject lines are to be filtered it should be done as part of a compound filter, e.g., subject line AND file size. If you are in any doubt avoid doing it!

One final note of caution when it comes to exclusion filtering. If the context of the DSAR specifically requests messages that would be automatically removed as part of the search strategy and exclusion filters just mentioned, and they are not covered by an exemption, then a controller must not exclude them. For example, a student may request automated emails because they want to reference the content of the messages to exercise a different data protection right (e.g., the right to rectification). Now we have all those key factors mentioned above, let's look at how you can document the

Identification Plan. The following steps will aid you in ensuring your identification plan is accurate and complete.

- Ensure the RoPA is up-to-date and accurate.
- Determine the data subject categories.
- Filter RoPA for current data sources
- Identify legacy data sources.
- Identify messaging systems.
- Identify raw data repositories.
- Identify relevant system owners.
- Develop keyword lists.
- Create taskings.
- Assign & track taskings.

Let's have a look at each of these in a little more detail...

**Ensure the RoPA is up-to-date and accurate:** The first, and most important, item on your identification plan is to confirm the Record of Processing Activities is accurate and up to date. If the RoPA is complete it will ensure no records are missed in the discovery process. Technically, this is not a task that should be started at the beginning of the DSAR process. It is something that should be conducted on a regular basis. We would recommend putting in place a monthly RoPA review whereby all heads of department are required to attest there are no new processing activities occurring within their business units. This attestation could also be augmented by an automated information asset discovery process.

**Determine data subject Categories:** The next step in the identification plan is to assess which data categories the data subject falls into. For example, a person making a DSAR request may be a customer and an employee, or they may now be a member of the public but have previously been an employee. By combining an up to date RoPA with correct data subject categorisation we are beginning to narrow down the places where we are required to go fishing for data!

**Filter RoPA for Current Data Sources (incl. 3rd Parties):** Now we have determined the data subject categories we can filter the RoPA to only the processing activities and, by proxy, the data sources that contain relevant material. If, for example, a data subject making a DSAR is not an employee there is no need to include the Human Resources Information System. Conversely, if the data subject is not a customer then there is no need to include the invoicing system or CRM.

Don't forget to consider external systems hosted by third parties. You might use a CRM tool like Hubspot, or an eCommerce platform like Shopify, and if the system contains personal data of a particular category of data subject, then, internal or external, it is in scope. It's more important to identify external sources as retrieving the data from a third party may take longer … especially if you didn't agree SLAs for DSAR response times at the start of the contract.

**Identify Legacy Data Sources:** When dealing with organisations that have been around for a while the person dealing with a DSAR may have to retrieve data stored on systems that are no longer operational. This situation can arise when an organisation upgrades their systems from old to new technology or switches from one application vendor to another. The older the organisation the more likely it is you will come across these legacy systems. If this information is not in your RoPA a good place to start is your IT department. Hopefully they will be maintaining such information in a configuration management database (or CMDB). The CMDB is essentially a list of all technology that is used in the organisation. If the data subject's personal data has been processed over several years some of their data may be in legacy systems. You will need to arrange with the custodian of these legacy systems to ensure the relevant data can be retrieved.

**Identify Messaging Systems (Email, IM, Message Boards):** In addition to legacy systems and specific applications personal data is often processed within an organisation's communication system. The most common is email, but organisations are rapidly expanding the way they communicate with each other, and several employ the use of messaging systems such as Yammer and Slack. Organisations may also use forums and internal message boards and might have set up WhatsApp (or equivalent) groups. Each of these messaging systems are in scope of a DSAR so processes must be in place to ensure this data can be extracted. Whilst we're on the subject of messaging systems. Some employees can forget themselves when using corporate messaging systems and can often make comments, about both customers and their colleagues, that could be damaging to an organisation's reputation should a data subject see them. It's good practice to ensure there is a policy in place to make certain employees know how to use these messaging systems appropriately. Remember, a data subject is entitled to see all comments made about them regardless of whether they are positive or negative.

**Identify Raw Data Repositories:** It is highly likely that personal data will find its way out of controlled systems of record and into 'raw data' repositories. Raw data repositories are your organisation's file systems and document libraries. You may use tools such as Teams, G-Suite or SharePoint to store data. For example, you may store client letters in PDF format in SharePoint. You may store annual consolidated employee performance and bonus reports in a management folder on your company file system. Wherever personal data is stored, it is still in scope of a DSAR. Make sure these repositories are also identified so they are included in your searches.

**Identify Audio / Visual Repositories:** Personal data in audio or visual form has become increasingly prevalent as more of our lives has moved online and internet bandwidth has made the use of audio / visual formats more realistic. What once took an age to download a single image has been replaced by an era of real-time hi-resolution video streaming with automatic transcription. controllers must be aware of how they process personal data in audio or visual form and ensure they have mechanisms to fulfil their data protection obligations when it comes to this type of material – including the right to access. Examples might include recording customer service calls, creation of digital IDs, CCTV footage and recording of video calls to support employee performance management.

**Identify System Custodians:** A system custodian is another term for the owner of a system, and they will facilitate the extraction of relevant personal data from this system. Some organisations may call this person the business owner or others could use the term information asset owner. This person's role should be recorded within the RoPA for ease of identification. If not within the RoPA it should be recorded within the CMDB or Service Management Tool, and at a minimum the role should be included in the system documentation. As a precursor to conducting any DSAR the system custodian should have processes and procedures in place to support the DSAR process. If you're a Data Protection Officer and you're not sure whether this is in place assign yourself a task to check this out. The main reason you need to identify System Custodians is because you're not going to be doing all the retrieval work yourself. The System Custodian will do this work. A DPO needs to have a way of assigning this work to a System Custodian and subsequently tracking the task until completion – hopefully within the required deadline!

**Develop Keyword Lists:** Keywords will be an important tool in ensuring the search is limited and doesn't pull in too much data. Keyword searches are discussed in more detail in a later section but, at a basic level, keywords and search criteria must be defined to ensure custodians know what to look for. Keywords also ensure searches are conducted in a consistent and repeatable manner each and every time. Most importantly, effective use of keywords can mean the difference between a few days of work and a few months! And finally don't forget to identify your exclusion keywords where appropriate.

**Create Tasking (use Templates where possible):** After a DPO has identified all the information described in the previous steps it's then time to create taskings. A predefined and tested tasking template will ensure the process of personal data retrieval runs smoothly. The tasking artefact will provide part of the audit trail should an organisation be investigated at a later date (e.g., if a data subject makes a complaint). It's therefore critical the taskings contain an appropriate level of detail to demonstrate searches were appropriate to the request. The content of a DSAR tasking will be discussed in more detail in a later section of this chapter.

**Assign & Track:** The final component of the identification plan is to assign and track its implementation. As the DPO you will need to keep on top of each task to check the output of searches is returned within an appropriate time frame to support the next steps in the DSAR process. Remember, in most cases the DSAR material needs to be issued to the data subject within 30 days, so it's important to give those conducting searches a shorter deadline. A timeframe of five to ten days to return initial unredacted findings would be good practice. DPOs should also consider the operational impacts, in particular the allocation of DSAR related tasks, when establishing deadlines. For example, if redaction, which will be discussed in a later chapter, is to be completed by the data custodian directly after the search, a longer deadline may be required than compared to a situation where redaction is completed centrally by other employees in the data protection team. The likelihood of queries and the possible return of incomplete or incorrect data should also be taken into consideration when determining deadlines.

There you have it - the identification plan in a nutshell. In the next few sections of this chapter, we shall delve into more details about some key aspects of the ID plan.

# Collection Instructions

Whilst much of the identification plan will stay with the DPO (or their delegate, the collection instructions will go out to each affected custodian. The collection instructions must, therefore, be clear as to what is required. The custodian must know this is not a request they can get around to eventually depending on how much other work is going on at the same time. They must be made aware there is a strict SLA for the retrieval task and that a failure to complete the task could result in regulatory censure for the organisation. It's in the DPO's interest to make sure data custodians are periodically reminded of the implications of missing subject access request SLAs. Ultimately, it's only going to result in increased workloads for the Data Protection team if DSARs are delivered late, or incomplete, and complaints then increase.

It's therefore useful to have a collection instructions template so nothing gets missed. The following example shows the items that are recommended for inclusion: -.

1. Title: Data Subject Access Request (DSAR) - Search Request
2. UID: Usually system generated but if not the DPO should provide a UID that doesn't include any personal data e.g., DSAR-SR-25052021-001
3. Status: e.g., Open, On-Hold, Closed, Awaiting Clarification, Cancelled
4. data subject Name: John Doe
5. Date Request Made: 25 May 2021
6. Date Assigned to Custodian: 26 May 2021
7. Request Deadline: 05 June 2021
8. System in scope of search: Human Resources Information System (HRIS) *Create a **unique** collection instruction for **each** system for improved tracking.
9. Data Custodian: Genghis Khan
10. Keywords List: *included keywords should be limited to those relevant to the specific system.

| Full Name | John David Doe |
| --- | --- |
| Candidate Number | REC01248974515 |
| Employee Number | UK3677864 |
| Date First Applied | 25 May 2017 |
| Start Date | 30 June 2017 |
| End Date | 25 May 2021 |

*Figure 9 - Keywords List*

11. <u>Search Criteria</u>:  See knowledge base article KB001245 for current instructions on how to search this system.
12. <u>Exclusion Criteria</u>: Exclude emails from the following mailboxes:

> noreply@foxredrisk.com
> reports@foxredrisk.com

13. <u>Approved Formats</u>: *.CSV, *.XLSX, *.PDF, *.JPG
14. <u>Secure Repository</u>: Please arrange with IT to transfer search material to the following secure SharePoint folder:

> e.g.,   https://foxredrisk.sharepoint.com/sites/DPO/DSAR/DSAR-25052021-001/DSAR-SR-25052021-001/c - Preserve Raw Material/

15. <u>Legal Hold</u>: Material identified using the keywords listed in this search request are to be placed on Legal Hold until further notice and are **NOT** to be destroyed when they reach the end of their retention period. For further details on Legal Hold procedures, please review the current Record Retention Policy.

16. <u>Point of Contact</u>: For any questions related to this request, please contact dpo@foxredrisk.com
17. <u>Special Instructions</u>: data subject has asked for all information held but has also specifically requested information about his performance review in Jan 2021.
18. <u>Nil Return</u>: A nil return is required to confirm searches were conducted but no material was identified.

If you can build the above tasking into your service management tool many of the items above can be generated automatically. Where there is an element of choice the use of input validation controls such as drop downs, check boxes, and date pickers is strongly recommended to ensure the request gets to the right person. If you don't have a Service Management Tool consider setting up a SharePoint library instead of going straight to the spreadsheet option. We know it's the easy option but over time that initial effort will make all the difference!

## Data Stored with Processors

Where some of your Processing activities are conducted by processors it is important to make sure each processor understands their role and responsibilities in the DSAR process. Remember, it's the controller on the hook for any enforcement action should the DSAR not be properly fulfilled.  It's incumbent upon the controller to make sure processors provide the personal data they hold in good time. That time frame needs to enable the controller to then provide the DSAR on time to the data subject. It's also worth noting that whilst processors are required to support a controller to fulfil their Data Protection obligations this does not mean they can't charge a controller for each DSAR they support. This may be baked into the cost of providing their service offering but is not always the case, and if you are in receipt of significant volumes of DSARs, a potentially unlimited charging regime could become very expensive. It is therefore important to include language in your contracts related to the fulfilment of DSARs – as we have said before … *caveat emptor!*

The contractual language should incorporate SLAs that state the time limit to report any DSARs made directly to the processor, and the time limit to provide the DSAR material when a request has been made. The language should also signpost an agreed procedure the processor must follow when conducting searches and the template that will be used by the controller to provide the search parameters. If possible, the language should explicitly confirm there will be no additional costs for processing DSARs.

## Keyword Searches

In the last section we briefly covered the need to create keyword lists and we will now look at keyword searches in more detail. If you think you're just going to whack the name of a data subject into a search tool and a full and complete set of data, covering just the requesting data subject, and nothing else, is going to miraculously appear then think again! When fulfilling a Data Subject Access Request good keyword searches are going to be your best friend!

Finding specific data on a specific data subject can be really difficult. For example, imagine your data subject is an employee and has been with the company for several years. They may be part of multiple internal mailing lists and they may have sent thousands, if not tens of thousands, of emails. Now imagine your data subject is referred to by others in emails in which they were neither sender nor recipient. Some may refer to the data subject by their first name, some by a nickname, some may use their initials, and some may use just their last name. Now imagine the person has a common name - David, Pierre, Mohammad, Sarah, Noor, or Isabelle. How do you sort out the wheat from the chaff? How do you know the Mohammed or Isabelle mentioned is the same Mohammed or Isabelle as the data subject? The short answer is with a fair degree of difficulty if you don't know what you're doing. The longer answer is with intelligent use of keywords you can narrow your searches considerably.

When creating keyword lists you should first collate the various identifiers attached to a data subject. For example, you may wish to include the following: -

1.  Email Address (john.doe@foxredrisk.com)
2.  First Name (John)
3.  Last Name (Doe)
4.  Known Nicknames (Johnny, Jonno, 'The Doe')
5.  Initials (JD)
6.  Employee or Customer Number (e.g. C123456)
7.  Date of Birth (20/05/2018)
8.  Other relevant dates (e.g. Employment Start/End date)

When you have the raw keywords, you can then use the most appropriate keywords for the system in question. For example, in an employee database it would be more appropriate to use an employee number than search for a name.   as it is very possible you could have two, or more, employees of the same name, especially in large organisations, and the same applies to CRMs or invoicing systems.

Where you are searching systems without a formal data structure, such as email or SharePoint, consider how you can eliminate false positives by the use of Boolean searches. A Boolean search uses operators such as 'AND', 'OR', and 'NOT' to limit, or sometimes expand, searches by combining a keyword with another search parameter.

There are other Boolean operators but 'AND', 'OR' and 'NOT' are the most commonly supported within application search tools.

'John' OR 'Jon' would return all content that contained either the word 'John' OR the word 'Jon'.

'John' AND 'Jon' would return only content that contained both 'John' AND 'Jon'. If the content only contained one keyword, it would not be returned in the search results.

'John' NOT 'John A' would return any record with the keyword 'John' but not where the string 'John' was followed by a space and the character 'A'. For example, a record with John Doe would be returned, but a record with 'John Anderton' or 'John Ambleside' would be filtered out of the search.

Boolean searches work even better alongside wildcards typically denoted by an asterisk '*' or a question mark '?'. The '?' wildcard is typically used to replace single characters in a search.

e.g., 's??n' could return 'Sean' or 'Sian'.

The * wildcard is typically used to expand a fragment of a search term.

e.g., 'Joh*' could return 'John', 'Johnny', 'Johnno'.

Boolean searches and wildcards can be used in combination to focus on very specific information. Take for example a search for the name John Doe where your organisation may have several employees named John. You know employees will not always be referred to by their full name, so a Boolean search can be used to eliminate as many other references to any old John where it can be reasonably deduced they are not the John that is the subject of the particular DSAR.

Here is an example of such a Boolean search: -:

'John' NOT ('John A' OR 'John B' OR 'John C' OR 'John E' OR 'John [keep adding letters from F to Y]' OR 'John Z')

In addition to using Boolean operators with keywords lists, one should also consider Boolean logic with other parameters such as key dates. For example, if the data subject became an employee on a particular date it would not be sensible to search prior to their first job application, however, be careful not to use their start date as material created as part of the application process would then be missed.

Using the search parameters 'C123456' AND '25 May 2018 - Today' would return only references to C123456 that occur after the 25 May 2018 and before the present date.

The same logic can be applied with customers. In both cases, time limiting searches will make searches quicker as the database won't need to work as hard. To improve the efficiency of your search processes consider recording such information in the relevant systems of records. So, in your HR Information System record the date the employee first applied for a role, and in your CRM, make a similar note in respect to the first contact with a customer or prospect.

Our final useful tip for searching relates to searching for names. If the system allows, add the name within speech marks with a space after the name e.g. "Catriona ". Search algorithms don't know that you are searching for names and so will be looking for the characters wherever they appear, including in other words. For example, "Ed" could appear in "last**ed**" and "Teri" could appear in "ma**teri**al". By adding the space practitioners can remove a high volume of false positive results.

These are just a few tips there are many other things that can be done with keywords to limit the amount of data returned from a search. Remember though the way searches can be performed will differ in each of your systems and search logic and nomenclature will vary. Build up a cheat sheet of key search criteria to make each future DSAR easier to manage.

This is not the end of keywords. We will revisit the topic later in the book, and in particular, how keywords are useful in the processing of material that is returned from searches.

## Inferred Data

Inferred data is data that is derived from other sources of non-personal data linked to the data subject to create a profile. Such profiles are often statistically derived using machine learning. For example, a data subject may have stated they are interested in basket weaving, their favourite food is pizza, and they own a dachshund dog, or they may have liked a post on a social media site by a journalist from a particular newspaper. A machine learning algorithm could potentially take these data points and determine the data subject is 91% likely to have a right-wing voting preference. This profile could then be used to target the data subject with targeted messaging to influence how they vote in an upcoming election or referendum. Despite the original data points not being personal data, anything inferred from these data points, is personal data and may be subject to disclosure. If you are in a jurisdiction where such data is disclosable, such as the UK/EU, then you must ensure the material forms part of your identification plan.

# Preserve

When a data subject has made a request, and the Personal Data has been collected from across the organisation, a controller now needs to ensure the data collected is preserved until the DSAR has been formally fulfilled. That is to say, the data subject has taken receipt of the DSAR bundle and any questions, complaints or litigation relating to the material have been concluded. Furthermore, as the initial material will be processed in a destructive way (e.g., by de-duplication and redaction) there is always the possibility of mistakes being made, such as over-zealous redacting of a document based on an incorrectly applied exemption. Given that some form of regulatory complaint, or litigation, can often follow-on from a DSAR, it is wise for a controller to make sure they can defend any treatment decisions by providing both redacted and unredacted versions of DSAR material to a relevant court, or data protection regulator, should it be lawfully requested. Notwithstanding the above the original material from which the DSAR material was extracted could be subject to automated data retention policies and could be deleted arbitrarily. What each of the issues described above lead to is a need for effective processes and procedures to ensure the DSAR material is preserved from deliberate, accidental, or malicious destruction before it can be provided to the data subject. In this section we will cover how preservation can be achieved.

## Creating a Safe Space

If you recall from the preparation phase of the Right to Access Fulfilment Model, we discussed the need to create a DSAR processing environment. In particular, the need for a place to securely store DSAR material whilst it is being processed. Hopefully this storage area has been set up and the relevant people have access, but now, it's an empty area. As more and more DSARs come in you will want to ensure that material from one DSAR does not get mixed up with another. You will also need to make certain that processed and unprocessed material don't get mixed up. To that end it's worth having a data structure in mind.

There are several different ways to store data in a file system so it can be easily retrieved. The modern method of structuring data is to place everything in one repository and tag different documents with relevant metadata before, or at the time, of placing it in the repository. Views are then created on top of this data that are tailored to different audiences. Tools such as SharePoint do this well and in certain circumstances this can be the ideal approach. For DSARs however, we do **NOT** recommend this method as it is highly likely material will get mixed up if tags are incorrectly applied. Whilst now a more outdated approach it is recommended a static folder structure is used that mirrors the RAFM phases, as per Figure 10 below. When the material from your searches is provided by the relevant system owners it should be added to the Preserve Folder. The raw files must then be set to "Read Only" and any "allow delete" options within the folder disabled. Setting to read only preserves the original material in the event it should be needed at a future point. It will also prevent accidental deletion or alteration. A copy of the material should be made and placed in the review folder ready for the first stage of processing in the treatment phase.

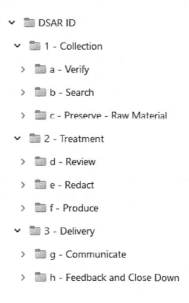

*Figure 10 - DSAR Folder Structure*

# Litigation Hold

You must not destroy evidence – it is illegal!

Some may assume if you have stumbled across material that is embarrassing, and would present the organisation in an unflattering light, that it can be simply deleted. Some may also be inclined to think if data falls outside of a retention period, but has yet to be deleted, that the material can be taken out of the scope of the DSAR. In both these cases this is incorrect, and in some jurisdictions, could also be against the law. For example, under the law of England and Wales, the Data Protection Act 2018 (Section 173) makes it a criminal offence for organisations to "*alter, deface, block, erase, destroy or conceal information with the intention of preventing disclosure*".

There is a principle in the legal world known as litigation, or legal, hold. This principle means that where an organisation assesses litigation may be "reasonably anticipated" data must be preserved to prevent evidence from becoming altered or destroyed. Whilst it doesn't necessarily follow that when someone makes a DSAR the request will be a precursor to litigation, DSARs can often be the first step a data subject makes before progressing an issue before the courts or making a complaint to their Data Protection regulator. In addition, where a current, or former, employee makes a DSAR the risk of this evolving into legal action is also more likely. It is therefore recommended in situations where information could be automatically, or deliberately, deleted after a DSAR has been made, that policies and procedures exist to ensure DSAR material is placed under litigation hold For example, if a person in the UK makes a DSAR about their employment record in the 5th year and 11th month of the record's existence, that material must be preserved so it isn't deleted at the six-year point[6]. Having procedures for litigation hold are particularly important where data resides in legacy systems and archives, or, where extensions to the 30-day rule have been applied and the chances of accidental deletion are increased.

# The Index File

Shortly after your search requests have been issued, you should then receive all the lovely personal data into your processing environment. Depending on the source of the material it's likely to come to you in lots of different files, and potentially lots of different formats. Much will come electronically but some could also be provided in physical form. As will become apparent in the next chapter, each physical and electronic document will need to go through the treatment phase, so it is good practice to have a way to keep track of what has been done to each file or document. A controller will need to consider how they can evidence all the relevant material requested by the data subject has been collected, treated, and communicated in a manner that is compliant with the relevant data protection legislation. For this purpose we recommend the creation of an index file.

An index file, at its simplest, is a separate document list of all the different files and some additional metadata related to each file. If you have an all singing all dancing e-Discovery tool it is highly likely indexing capability is built in. If not, and you're not ready to invest in specific or expensive tooling, you can produce an index semi-manually using nothing more complicated than a spreadsheet tool such as Excel. This file should be kept in the highest level of your DSAR file structure so it can be found and updated easily. The naming convention should also include the same unique ID as the DSAR itself (e.g. Index – DSAR-SR-25052021-001.xlsx).

So, what should be included in the index file? Here is our list:

- Name (or Unique ID) of data subject
- Search Criteria e.g., the terms used to collect the material.

---

[6] UK employment law requires some employment records be retained for six years.

- Initial Bundle Hash
- Final Bundle Hash
- File information (record this information for each individual file):
  - File Names
  - File Type
  - Stage of Processing (i.e. the current sub-stage of the RAFM such as "*Review*" or "*Redact*" or "*Communicate*")
  - Contains third party data – Yes / No
  - Redaction Required – Yes / No
  - Exemptions Applied – Yes / No
  - Conversion required – Yes / No
  - Comments/Notes
- Delivery to data subject Date
- Destruction Date

Don't worry at this stage if some of the index headings don't make sense as many relate to topics we are yet to cover. Don't worry though, all will be accounted for in the next few chapters! At this stage, we just want you to get an idea of the information that could be in an index file. The list is not exhaustive, and you may wish to include other information. For example, you may wish to include a point of contact next to each file should you have an issue (e.g., a file is, or becomes, corrupted). You may also wish to record the dates each stage of processing was completed for continuous improvement purposes. You may wish to split your index file into multiple worksheets to manage physical and electronic files separately. Ultimately, the index file is there to aid you in completing the DSAR process as efficiently as possible, whilst also providing a useful way of demonstrating that the controller has complied with the data subject's request.

## Hashing

In chapter five we briefly touched upon the potential need for hashing tools and how they can provide a mechanism to confirm whether material has been altered in some way. In this section we will discuss how hashing can be applied to the collected data and how hashing may also be used in future phases of the RAFM. In many cases hashing is overkill.  This section has been included for situations where it might be useful, for evidentiary purposes, to demonstrate material has not been tampered with and can therefore be verified as genuine by the ultimate recipient.

There are two specific use cases we will cover where hashing may be of some benefit. The first use case relates to sending highly sensitive DSAR material through an untrusted third party using physical media (e.g., a USB storage drive / DVD) or via an internet accessible portal. Both of these systems must be protected by some form of authentication process. However, this does not mean a third-party actor cannot break the authentication mechanism and potentially manipulate or delete material before it is sent to the data subject – there is no such thing as 100% secure. Whilst hashing won't prevent unauthorised access it will provide a way to alert the data subject that unauthorised manipulation and/or deletion has occurred in transit. The process would require the material to be hashed prior to delivery and the hash value being communicated to the data subject via a different channel to the DSAR material (e.g., if material is sent in the post, send the hash value via email). The data subject could hash the material on receipt and the hash value of the received material should be the same as the hash value in the associated communication.

Whilst hashing provides an extra level of protection, by confirming the data is genuine and unaltered, the primary drawback is it heavily relies on the data subject being sufficiently technically competent to re-hash the material on receipt. This is not usually the case. If, on evaluating whether hashing is something you feel is a necessary step consideration must be given to including suitable guidance, such as a video tutorial, on how a data subject should validate the hashes upon receipt.

The second use case is for internal purposes to support the chain of custody. In a similar way to the first use case this could be where the DSAR material is highly sensitive, likely to end up in litigation, or contains material that might have a negative reputational impact on the controller. For example, a data protection practitioner may need support from those working in the business to review, deduplicate and redact the DSAR material. One of those assisting may find something within the material that is damaging to the controller or its employees – or perhaps even themselves! This person may choose to delete, or amend, the material to prevent the material reaching the data subject, and this is where hashing can help prevent unauthorised alteration of files. Hashing the material at each stage of the DSAR process will generate an audit trail that can be used to confirm the material has not been altered without appropriate authorisation. In addition to any internal control mechanisms, an assurance body such as an internal or external audit function, could also use the hash values to independently verify the DSAR process is operating with integrity. This use case is simpler to implement than the first use case above as all elements of the process are internal to the controller and do not involve the data subject.

As mentioned earlier, both scenarios are likely to be overkill in most cases, but if you do need to demonstrate that files have not been manipulated or altered how do you hash a file, or files, in practice? There are a few options but here are two. The first is using the PowerShell functionality built into the Microsoft Windows Operating System, and the second is using a hashing application such as HashMyFiles. To demonstrate we will look at the PowerShell option for two primary reasons. First, you don't need to install anything new to use PowerShell if you are running Windows 10 or above, and second, third-party applications will typically have documentation that is maintained by the application developers so there is no need to "re-hash" it here (see what we did?!)

# Hashing using MS Windows PowerShell (Windows 10/11)

- Identify the **full** folder location of the files you wish to hash e.g., "*C:\Folder with files to hash\*"
- Open PowerShell as an Administrator by

  o Clicking the Windows button and typing "PowerShell".
  o Right click on the PowerShell icon and choose to "Run as Administrator".

- A PowerShell terminal window should open.
- In the terminal paste your version of the following command, amending the algorithm with hashing algorithm you wish to use (e,g. MD5 or SHA256), the file location you wish to hash (*C:\Folder with files to hash\*) and the location you wish the file hashes to be stored *(D:\Hashes.csv)*.

  o "*Get-FileHash -Algorithm MD5 -Path (Get-ChildItem "C:\Folder with files to hash\*.*" -Recurse -force) | export-csv D:\Hashes.csv*"
- Open CSV file to review content and you should see something like the image below:

| | Algorithm | Hash | Path |
|---|---|---|---|
| 1 | Algorithm | Hash | Path |
| 2 | MD5 | C8394375B4B7FEE1178D71DDCF9E76F5 | C:\Folder with files to hash\UnhashedFile1.pdf |
| 3 | MD5 | E7C2C72F6290BC50B972DCC6A67BCAAE | C:\Folder with files to hash\UnhashedFile2.pdf |
| 4 | MD5 | 9506B84A4F9B427C42E3CA256E634FCE | C:\Folder with files to hash\UnhashedFile3.pdf |
| 5 | MD5 | 62CCA4F4B8A61EDAE97D672596D1216B | C:\Folder with files to hash\UnhashedFile4.pdf |

*Figure 11 - Hashed File Output*

To check if anything has changed at a later date simply follow the same steps used to originally hash the files and compare the output. If you are using a spreadsheet to compare the hashes a compare formula that checks if two cells have the same value (e.g., =B3=C3) could be used to visually highlight any differences. As you can see in Figure 12 the first hash is different which confirms the hashed file has been altered.

| | A | B | C | D | |
|---|---|---|---|---|---|
| 1 | Algorithm | Hash(Original) | Hash (Last checked) | Changed? | Path |
| 2 | MD5 | C8394375B4B7FEE1178D71DDCF9E76F5 | 4E4A1DEF84F0B1871F0A65464C32776C | FALSE | C:\Folder with |
| 3 | MD5 | E7C2C72F6290BC50B972DCC6A67BCAAE | E7C2C72F6290BC50B972DCC6A67BCAAE | =B3=C3 | C:\Folder with |
| 4 | MD5 | 9506B84A4F9B427C42E3CA256E634FCE | 9506B84A4F9B427C42E3CA256E634FCE | TRUE | C:\Folder with |
| 5 | MD5 | 62CCA4F4B8A61EDAE97D672596D1216B | 62CCA4F4B8A61EDAE97D672596D1216B | TRUE | C:\Folder with |

*Figure 12 - Hashed File Comparison*

The additional benefit of using PowerShell over a third-party application is that further automation can be applied to this process. For example, an initial hashing file could be automatically added to the folder at the start of the DSAR. Furthermore, the creation of hashing files could be automated at each stage of the process. Hashes at the beginning of a new RAFM phase could be automatically checked against the output of the previous stage, to confirm nothing has been missed, deleted or altered, with alerts triggered if the hash values do not match suggesting unauthorised activity has occurred.

# Summary

The focus of this chapter was to work through the collection phases of the Right to Access Fulfilment Model. Firstly, we looked at verification. We considered how to ensure we have the correct data subject and how to check they are who they say they are. We looked at how to know what the data subject is requesting and the importance of checking we have verified which legislation may be valid in addition to primary data protection legislation.

Secondly, we took a deep dive into searches to ensure we are collecting all the data subject's relevant material and excluding as much irrelevant material as possible. We walked through the stages of creating an Identification Plan and also discussed handling data held with processors. We also explained how to carry out effective keyword searches.

Finally, we reviewed how the collected material can be preserved. We discussed the potential need to place material into litigation hold, and how to create a file structure and indexes to ensure the DSAR process operates efficiently. We also briefly discussed scenarios in which file hashing may be useful in ensuring DSAR material is not accidentally or deliberately altered.

So, now we have collected the DSAR material in our access controlled DSAR processing environment, it's now time to move on to the next stage of the RAFM – the Treatment phase.

# Chapter Seven – Treatment Phase

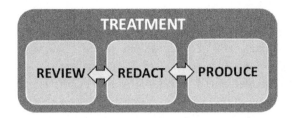

*Figure 13 - Treatment Phase*

Well done on making it this far, we're now at the penultimate phase! In this chapter we are going to take all the raw material collected from across your organisation and get it ready to provide to the data subject. Welcome to the Treatment phase of the RAFM!

The three sub-components of the RAFM treatment phase are **Review, Redact** and **Produce**. In the Review section we will look at how to further minimise the material collected thus far. We will examine how to identify third party data and how to identify and apply exemptions. We will also briefly consider the intersection of intellectual property law and its impact on DSARs. Finally, we will look at situations where seeking legal advice may be prudent as a result of the content found when reviewing the DSAR material.

In the Redact section we will look at the end-to-end redaction process, walking through each step and highlighting how automation can improve efficiency and accuracy. We will also explore redaction of audio and visual files and the different techniques controllers can use to process non-text-based personal data.

In the Produce section we be primarily focussed on putting the DSAR and supplementary material together into a pack ready for onward communication to the data subject.

OK, on we go!

# Review

Let's set the scene. You've sent your search requests out across the business, and they have all come back. Sat within your DSAR folder structure lies several terabytes of data! There are 3.6million emails, 400,000 Word documents, several folders each containing 5,000 images and then there is a year of CCTV footage. You can't just hand this material over to the data subject, it all needs to be individually checked, assessed and treated. You do the maths and work out it's going to take you six years to go through it all – and that's if you don't take a break! Then you wake up and realise it's all just a horrible nightmare!! Well, we hope it is.

If this is the scenario you are facing, there is something seriously broken with your organisation's information governance and this book is only going to get you so far. Hopefully, though, after working your way through the last chapter's recommendations, you are working with a significantly smaller overall dataset. It's now time to review the material to ensure only relevant material, not covered by an exemption, is provided to the data subject. In this section we will discuss how to review the raw data to reduce the size of the dataset and remove duplicate material. This will save time and effort later. With the material reduced we will then discuss how to identify appropriate exemptions. This will then lead into another sub-process of the treatment phase, the redact sub-process. Occasionally, DSARs throw up complex or sensitive issues so we will end the review section with a discussion on when it might be appropriate to seek external legal advice.

## Lawful Basis for Processing

Before we go into the detail of the treatment phase, we want to take a minute to remind you that processing of personal data generally requires a lawful basis for processing. During the following sections you will be introduced to techniques that support the DSAR process, such as automated redaction, transcription, facial recognition and voice matching. These tools may support the DSAR process but are most likely implemented for other reasons e.g., improving customer service. Each is a processing activity and as such requires a lawful basis to be in place prior to processing. Some of the techniques may also process special category data and require additional technical and organisational controls to be put in place. Some processing, such as the use of machine learning or emergent artificial intelligence, are highly likely to meet the threshold for a full data protection impact assessment prior to implementation. With these examples in mind, if you implement tools make sure their operation is compliant with in-scope data protection legislation.

# Reduction and De-Duplication

When a data protection practitioner first begins the review stage of a DSAR they may find they are overwhelmed with the enormity of the task ahead of them. They may find masses of material that is not relevant to the data subject or is duplicated many times. Practitioners could find that documents contain a data subject's personal data, but the content doesn't relate to the data subject. They might find they are faced with thousands of emails and instant messages where the data subject is simply cc'd to a conversation relating to someone else, or they are included simply because of the role they hold in an organisation. Similarly, there will be email chains that contain the same content repeatedly as the chain gradually gets bigger. There will be document templates where the data subject is identified as holding a role or is the point of contact for issues. These are just a few examples of the material you may need to wade through but there are many more. When faced with this irrelevant or duplicated material you will need a set of guidelines that help determine when it is, and is not, ok to remove material. Here are a few points you might want to consider when creating your own guidelines:

- How to treat business-related emails and messages not related to the data subject but do include their name/email address
- How to treat business-related reports, meeting minutes and other documents not related to the data subject but do include their name/email address.
- How to treat email chains, e.g., supplying only the final chain and any forks instead of every single email as the chain builds
- How to treat duplicate material provided by two different data sources
- Removing emails footers, manually or automatically
- How to treat system access logs
- How to treat audio or visual material

When creating the guidelines, it is also useful to consider the potential differing data subject profiles. For example, it may be appropriate to remove certain content when the data subject is an employee but not when they are a customer. When applying such logic, it's important to remember the data subject may fall into more than one category. If this is the case, you will need to determine which set of guidelines is most appropriate.

It is also imperative to ensure that guidelines are applied contextually. If a data subject has been very specific about what they want, and this material isn't covered by an exemption, then it is less likely it would be appropriate to use subjectivity. For example, if you have determined in your guidelines that standard practice is to not include system access logs, but rather explain that the data subject's name appears in them, but the data subject is explicitly asking for access to these logs, then these logs should be provided. Remember internal guidelines don't override the law!

The reduction and de-duplication guidelines controllers create should also support your DSAR communication templates which are discussed more in the next chapter. This should help you formulate text related to personal data that appears but has not been included in the DSAR material. For example, in the context of a DSAR related to an employee you may decide to reduce the dataset by removing material where the data subject's personal data is included as a recipient to business-related emails. This exclusion should be explained in the response letter sent to the data subject using a form of words like those described below:

"*Your name appeared as part of your business email address in 7,230 email and instant messages. The content of these emails did not relate directly to you and are confidential in nature and so have not been included in our response to your DSAR*".

By applying some common sense, repeatable reduction, and de-duplication guidelines you should be able to reduce the effort needed to further process the DSAR material. Depending on the systems you have available you may also be able to automate some of this work. If you do decide to go down the path of automation, be sure to regularly test any automation doesn't inadvertently remove material the data subject is entitled to access.

## Identifying Third Party Personal Data

When fulfilling a DSAR it is a very common occurrence to find the data subject's personal data is intermingled with that of others. The data subject's name may appear in meeting minutes, in performance appraisal scoring tables or in lists of exam results. The data subject may be discussed in relation to their parent or their children. They may also be discussed by a third party in the context of a reference or a medical examination. In most cases, even when the third party is already known to the data subject, third party personal data will not fall within the scope of a DSAR and so it must be stripped from the material sent to the data subject. The primary exception to this is where the third party has expressly given permission and there will be more on this later in the section. It should also be noted that content created by a third party in relation to a data subject could also render the third party as identifiable.

The practitioner tasked with processing the DSAR should therefore review the material to identify third parties and third-party content. When identifying third parties it's important to consider not just names but also roles and communication details e.g., email and telephone numbers. This is because when we move to the redaction phase anything that could potentially reidentify the third party will need to be removed. For example, when it comes to job titles there is generally only going to be one person who holds the role of Head of Finance (or similar); the same applies with phone numbers and handles.

We briefly mentioned above that a third party can give permission for their personal data to be made identifiable. This is permitted under many data protection laws, but disclosure needs to be considered in context. For example, a teacher at a school who has put their name to a child's school report is unlikely to have an issue having their name in the report should it now appear in a DSAR. Conversely, the same teacher may not want their name associated with a private conversation about a safeguarding issue which is not covered by an exemption. There may also be times where the data subject is aware something has been, or is likely to be, withheld. A good example of this may be where a confidential reference has been provided by a third party during a hiring process. The data subject may be unsuccessful in their application and could put in a DSAR to ascertain whether the reference had a negative impact on the hiring decision. Under EU and UK data protection legislation confidential references are exempt from disclosure. That said, a controller can ask the relevant third party, in this case the provider of the reference, if they would be willing to disclose the reference anyway.

There are a myriad of different scenarios where proactive disclosure or requesting third party consent to disclose is appropriate, and equally where disclosure of third-party information would be a very bad idea. As such the controller should create guidelines that cover common scenarios and should consider:

- When proactive disclosure is appropriate and to which data subjects this proactive disclosure applies
- When it is optional to request consent from a third party
- When it would be mandatory to request consent from a third party
- When third party consent will not be requested

As per the previous section any decisions relating to third party disclosure, where appropriate, should be communicated to the data subject. Where a controller is decides not to contact a third party to request consent, the controller should be able to justify that decision. Having a justification is important as it is possible the failure to request consent may give rise to the data subject making a complaint to a data protection regulator.

# Identifying & Applying Exemptions

When you have removed as much of the duplicate, non-relevant and third-party material as possible you should be left with material that directly relates to the data subject. The next stage of the review process is to go through this material and identify whether any exemptions should be applied. An exemption, in its simplest form is a means by which a controller can lawfully withhold the information they hold on a data subject. Exemptions exist because the law needs to balance the data subject's right to access their personal data with a controller's need to process that data effectively and within the scope of any other legislation to which they must comply.

When it comes to relying on exemptions in the context of the right to access controllers need to think about their specific purpose. For example, under UK and EU GDPR some exemptions are based on the purpose itself, whilst others only apply if fulfilling the right to access would have a negative effect on, or prevent necessary, processing. Whichever situation applies it's important to understand that exemptions can't be used as a catch-all solution. Exemptions also can't be used to minimise the effort of processing the DSAR, or to act as a crutch for excessive processing or data retention.

So how can a controller identify exemptions? Exemptions will vary depending on the jurisdiction in which a controller operates, by type of organisation and often by sector too. For example, a law enforcement organisation will be able to apply different exemptions than a social media company and a law firm will be able to apply different exemptions than a public sector organisation such as the NHS. The first step is for a controller to go through the data protection legislation that applies to them and identify the exemptions they are permitted to apply. The next step is to break down their DSARs by data subject type, work through the most common documents that appear in those DSARs and pre-emptively identify material that would fall under each specific exemption. Finally, it is also useful to workshop likely scenarios that might affect a controller and determine which exemptions might apply in each case. Then, in a similar way to the approach carried out in the prior sections on reduction and de-duplication and third parties, the controller should document exemption guidelines, broken down by either document type or scenario. These guidelines should state:

- Unique ID
- Scenario
- Applicable material
- Applicable data subjects
- Exemptions that may apply including the reference to the source legislation.
- Justification for applying the exemption.
- Whether the exemption is mandatory or optional
- Situations where the exemption should not be applied.
- Useful search keywords

Let's look at an example of an exemption guideline in more detail:

| | |
|---:|---|
| **Unique ID** | DSAR-EXEM-012 |
| **Scenario** | Redundancy Proceedings |
| **Applicable Material** | Documents and communications relating to the redundancy proceedings. |
| **Applicable Data Subjects** | Employees |
| **Applicable Exemptions** | UK DPA18. Sch 2, Part 4, Para 22 |
| **Justification** | Disclosure is likely to cause distress to |

| | |
|---|---|
| | wider employees prior to formal announcement of planned redundancies. |
| **Mandatory/Optional** | Mandatory |
| **Exceptions** | After formal announcement of redundancy proceedings have been made. Consult with Head of HR to confirm. |
| **Search Keywords** | redundancy, [redundancy codeword], consultation, appeal, redundancy, layoffs, termination, job loss, severance package, employment termination, workforce reduction, downsizing, rightsizing |

*Figure 14 - Exemption Schedule*

By applying some common sense and repeatable guidelines you should be able to reduce the effort needed to identify and apply the most likely exemptions to the DSARs you receive. By using common keywords related to the topic you should also be able to quickly find relevant material within the DSAR. If you're unsure how to create exemption guidelines, or don't have an in-house data protection capability, it may be useful to bring in a consultant to assist in pulling some guidelines together. In more complicated scenarios a controller may feel more comfortable seeking formal legal advice. Don't try to bluff your way through - if the data subject complains you are only going to make more work for yourself in the long run.

# Identifying Intellectual Property & Copyright Issues

The final core consideration in the review sub-process is that of intellectual property and copyright. During the review of the DSAR material it may become apparent that some items could be considered intellectual property. Intellectual property (IP), also defined as "creations of the mind", can include things such as patents, copyrights, trademarks or trade secrets. IP can also include images and designs, books, and other artistic works. The key point is that items that fall within the definition of intellectual property usually have restrictions on their use and distribution.

An in-depth discussion on intellectual property rights is outside the scope of this book. Controllers, however, do need to ensure that before they copy or distribute any material that they understand the intellectual property rights that apply. If in doubt, legal advice from an intellectual property law specialist is recommended. When it is understood which material has intellectual property rights attached, guidelines should be documented to ensure the material is treated according to those rights.

## Seeking Legal Advice

When reviewing the DSAR material a data protection practitioner may come across material they feel exposes the controller to legal risk. In general terms this legal risk may fall into two broad categories. The first category relates to the DSAR process itself or a lack of clarity regarding the controller's data protection obligations. Examples of which are as follows:

- Complex or excessive DSARs
- Disclosure of third-party data
- How to correctly apply exemptions
- Intellectual property or copyright issues
- Changes to data protection legislation
- Controller's legal obligations (e.g., issues relating to national security)
- Disputes and complaints relating to material already disclosed or withheld.

In such cases, where there is a lack of internal expertise, it may be appropriate to seek specialist legal advice from a practice that specialises in data protection law.

The second category of legal risk is where the DSAR material does not highlight any issues with the controller's data protection obligations but instead highlights exposure to other legal risk. Examples of which are as follows:

- Evidence of bullying or discrimination towards the data subject
- Material that could cause the controller significant reputational damage.
- Evidence of an employee admitting criminal liability for an act conducted in their role as an employee of the controller.
- Evidence of an employee admitting criminal liability for an act independent of their role as an employee of the controller
- Evidence of minor or gross misconduct by an employee
- Evidence of inappropriate workplace relationships
- Evidence of safeguarding issues, e.g., issues related to child protection or domestic violence.

In cases where issues such as those listed above are found there needs to be a process to appropriately bring this to the attention of senior management. This then allows a decision to be taken as to whether legal advice should be sought. We can't tell you whether you should or shouldn't take legal advice. What we will say, is whilst controllers may be dissuaded by the costs associated with taking legal advice, the cost of taking a course of action without understanding the legal implications could be significantly higher!

# Redact

In its very basic form redaction is the removal of sensitive material from a document rendering it irrecoverable, whilst at the same time retaining material that the intended recipient is authorised to view. In this section we will discuss the practical elements of the redaction process. This is to ensure that redaction is administered effectively, and sensitive material isn't inadvertently shared with the wrong person. Knowing how to redact a document accurately is a key skill for anyone involved in the DSAR process. Anyone who has been involved in fulfilling DSARs will know that an abundance of sensitive material can be uncovered. As the items listed in the 'seeking legal advice' section highlight, such sensitive material, if improperly disclosed, could expose a controller to high levels of legal risk. Even if the material doesn't expose a controller to legal risk, it could still cause significant distress to one or more data subjects. It's therefore important to ensure that material is redacted effectively before it is sent.

## The Redaction Process

So, what is the redaction process? The following steps are our recommended approach for tackling text-based documents. We will then cover audio / visual formats in the next section:

- Make digital copies of the material.
- Confirm location of sensitive material
- Collate reasons for applying redactions.
- Redact the material.
- Check all sensitive material has been redacted.
- Convert redacted document to a secure format.
- Test that redacted material cannot be recovered.

Let's have a look at each of the above steps in more detail...

**Make digital copies of the material**: Before applying any redactions, it is a good idea to compile all the material into a topic-specific PDFs and apply an optical character recognition (OCR) process to any document that has been scanned from a physical file. A copy of these PDFs should also be made. The reason for making an OCR-enabled PDF is to support automation of the redaction process, whilst at the same time making copies will mean you have a "clean" version for audit and review purposes. In consolidating all the material into themed documents redactions can be applied in multiple places with ease and exempted material is less likely to be missed.

**Confirm location of sensitive material**: Next, check the document and confirm the location of any of the sensitive material types identified during the review process. These sensitive material types relate to third party data, data covered by exemptions and data covered by intellectual property rights. If you have created guidelines to support your review process, you could use relevant keywords to aid in locating such material.

**Collate reasons for applying redactions**: As you confirm the locations of sensitive data you should collate a list of all the reasons that redaction will apply. This list serves two purposes. Firstly, the list gives you an audit trail you can use should a DSAR become a complaint. A complaint may come several weeks, or months, after you have sent the DSAR to the data subject and by this point you may not remember why the redaction was applied. Having a list can be a useful memory-jogging tool. Secondly, a template list could spin off the guidelines created in the review section and might look like this:

| Scenario | Document Name | Pages applied |
|---|---|---|
| Third Parties | DS-Emails.pdf | All |
| | DS-IMs.pdf | All |
| Redundancy | DS-Emails.pdf | 24-48, 310, 315-320 |
| Legal Professional Privilege | DS-document-003.pdf | 20-25 |

*Figure 15 - Redaction Schedule*

**Redact the material**: Whilst we recommend following a digital redaction process, we want to first recognise that some practitioners prefer to print out material into a physical format and apply a physical redaction method, e.g., using thick marker pen on both sides of a sheet of paper. For the purposes of this book, however, we will focus only on digital redaction.

When conducting digital redaction, it is useful to carry out the process in three passes. The first pass is an automated pass where standard material is automatically redacted. This first pass could also be supported by dictionaries of key words and key phrases built up from earlier reviews. The next pass is a semi-automated pass where repeated material is identified for redaction as the practitioner moves through the document. Upon finding the first occurrence of an item the practitioner then performs a search to find all the other locations where the same term exists. The practitioner then automatically applies redaction to each occurrence. This is particularly useful for names, telephone numbers and email addresses. The third pass is then a fully manual pass. This is where the practitioner goes through the material and manually redacts content that hasn't been caught under the previous two passes. Content in the third pass is more likely to be contextual and will likely need subjective review that, at time of writing at least, is outside the capabilities of most automated redaction tools.

**Check all sensitive material has been redacted**: Ok, so technically there is a fourth redaction pass. This final pass is a Quality Control (QC) pass and usually involves at least one additional set of eyes. Even after processing many DSARs over the years the old adage that it's very difficult to spot your own mistakes still rings true. We also find that, as a data protection practitioner, you may not necessarily have sufficient knowledge of the content to catch all the material that requires redacting.

**Convert redacted document to a secure format**: When all the redaction passes have been completed, the file should be saved in a format that ensures the material cannot be unredacted. The file should also be saved using a format that can be opened by the data subject without the requirement for exotic or paid software. We recommend a PDF file as this is a very common format and most internet browsers support this format. We also recommend password protecting the file with a complex password of 15 characters or more.

**Test that redacted material cannot be recovered**: Prior to sending the material tests should be conducted to confirm that redacted material cannot be recovered. Depending on your redaction software it may be possible to open the PDF file in Word, remove the black rectangles covering text and re-expose the original material. It may also be possible to derive the material indirectly from information embedded in the document during the optical character recognition (OCR) phase. If you are particularly concerned about either of these issues you can print the redacted documents out and then rescan the documents as a new PDF without going through an OCR process. Please note, when rescanning in this way, you may cause the PDF file size to increase dramatically. If you do find you have large PDF files you can alter the settings on your document scanner to find an appropriate setting that balances readability with file size.

Now you have a set of redacted PDFs you can move onto the production stage which we will discuss in the next section. For most people the above steps will typically be enough to redact the material they hold. For others there will be items such as call recordings and CCTV that will need to be processed using other tools and techniques discussed in the next section.

# Redacting Audio & Visual Material

Redacting audio and visual material is somewhat more technical than redacting text-based files. It can be made even more challenging when the files are in a proprietary file format that can only be accessed using specialist licensed software. With that said, if the data subject's personal data is contained in audio or visual files then it is possible these files will fall within the scope of their DSAR. Controllers, therefore, need to have tools and processes in place to provide this personal data in a format the data subject can access.

Most audio and visual redaction can now be done with off-the-shelf video editing software. Tools such as Da Vinci Resolve (free), Hit Film (freemium) or Adobe Premiere (paid) can easily do the job. Video and audio editing is, however, a topic that could cover several books and what works in one piece of editing software may not necessarily work in another. So, whilst it's not in the scope of this book to cover audio, video, or photo editing in any meaningful way, we still want to give some practical advice so you can get the best out of your chosen audio/visual editor. If you combine our guidance, with online tutorials from your video editor provider, you shouldn't go too far wrong.

In the following sections, we'll break down how to process audio/visual material. Firstly, processing of audio only files and then video and images both with and without audio. In both cases we will work on the assumption that the audio or video material falls within the scope of the DSAR and is not being excluded in its entirety by one or more exemptions. We will accept the request for the footage is reasonable and we will also assume, for the purposes of these examples, that we have verified the identity of the data subject.


## Processing Audio File Formats

Audio can be used in many ways. Business meetings may be recorded by a secretary to support the production of minutes. A data subject may request a performance management or disciplinary meeting be recorded. A witness statement could be recorded too. The most prevalent use for audio only in a commercial setting, however, is call-recording and so we will use call recordings as a case study to work through the process of how audio files can be made "DSAR-ready".

The first step is to confirm you have the right data subject. This could be done in one of four ways which gradually get more technical. The first, relatively easy way, is to verify with the data subject which telephone number they used when they made calls and search your call recording software for any calls from this number. However, this does not always work as the data subject may have withheld their number on some, or all, of the calls. Where this is the case acquiring the date and time of calls can help narrow the search. The next approach is to review the organisation's Customer Relationship Management (CRM) software. Good practice is to log calls with customers into a CRM to maintain a record of all customer interactions. By checking the CRM, the retriever can narrow down the searches to those specific times even if the caller withheld their number. Again, this is not foolproof as there may be times when the CRM was not updated after a customer made a call. The next option will depend on the sophistication of the call recording software. Some call recording software can carry out automatic transcription of calls. This transcription is then added to a searchable database that also links to an audio file of the call. Where such a feature exists text-based searches can be carried out. For example, it is highly likely t the data subject was referred to by name during the call. Now again, this is not foolproof and automatic transcription solutions can often mis-transcribe words. If you have additional context to a call e.g., it related to a specific complaint, this context could be used to further narrow down the number of calls. The fourth option is highly technical and involves using a sample of the data subject's voice e.g., from a verified phone call. That sample can then be used in the analysis of all the call recordings to ascertain whether the data subject's voice is present. Again, this option is not foolproof but combined with other methods could be used to narrow the amount of material that you will need to sift through.

When processing audio from a proprietary system you will first need to ascertain whether the file needs to be converted into a common format. Two of the most common formats are Wave (*.wav) and MPEG Layer 3 (*.mp3). Where possible it's best to work with mp3 files as these have much smaller file sizes. Ideally, when procuring call recording software, the ability to export to *.wav or *.mp3 should have been part of the must have feature list, but if not, you may need to work with the software vendor, or worst-case scenario rig a 3.5mm cable from the headphone to the microphone socket on a laptop and re-record the material. This is far from ideal as this would need to be conducted in real time.

When the recording is in a usable format create a working copy. This is essential as the editing process can sometimes crash – especially when editing large files. Before you start editing the file you may want to consider applying a denoising filter to the audio to help you better understand what is being said. You may also wish to apply automatic transcription to the file to get a better understanding of the content. The transcription can then aid in finding material that needs to be redacted.

After you have identified the material that needs to be redacted you can choose to apply "cuts" to the audio file. Most editors have different cut tools. There are cut tools that will retain a period of silence in the deleted sections, and this is commonly known as a "straight" cut. The alternative is a "time-shift" or "ripple" cut. These cuts will remove the deleted audio completely and paste together the two sections of audio on either side. We recommend a straight cut over ripple cuts as it makes it clear to the listener that audio has been removed. An optional step is to include an audio section at the beginning of the file that explains the file has been provided as part of a DSAR. This can clarify where exemptions have been applied and include a pointer to a document that explains which exemptions have been used. This doesn't have to be recorded anew every single time. The audio could be created in a separate file and appended to the beginning of each audio file as required. When the audio processing has been completed the file should be saved as a clean mp3 file ready for communication to the data subject.

In the above example a controller has determined a copy of the audio file should be be made available to the data subject. This is not the only option, and they could choose to provide a transcription of the audio file content instead. If practitioners are considering going down the transcript only route caution should be given to relying solely on automated transcription. These solutions are prone to high error rates, especially if they have not been trained on a specific person's voice. The automated transcription process should always be a first pass supported by human review. Redaction of the transcription should also be conducted by checking the audio and confirming the redaction is supported by the audio file content. It's also worth noting if the transcript is questioned as being inaccurate, and the data subject makes a successful complaint to a regulator, a controller may find themselves subject to enforcement action.

## Processing Visual File Formats

Just as audio can be used in many ways across an organisation, so too can visual material. Visual material can take the form of video, with or without audio, and imagery. Examples of video can include CCTV, screen recording, recording of online meetings or recording of training sessions. It may also take the form of promotional materials such as corporate videos. Examples of imagery could include photographs taken at corporate events, images used for ID cards or material posted on a controller's website. It could also include x-rays or 3D CT scans. The most prevalent use for video recording in a commercial setting, however, is CCTV and so we will use CCTV as a case study to work through the process of how a video file can be made "DSAR-ready".

As we did in the call recording example, we must first identify the personal data of the data subject within the CCTV footage. This could be the data subject themselves or they could be in a vehicle. When it comes to CCTV typically the data subject, or third-party party acting on their behalf, will have explicitly made a request for such footage. If they haven't already done so it is useful to go back to the data subject and clarify the dates, times, and locations of cameras in which they believe they have been captured. An alternative approach could be to use technology such as automatic number plate recognition (ANPR) or facial recognition provided this capability is already implemented in a lawful way.

After identifying the footage that contains the relevant personal data, the next step is to export that footage from the CCTV system and import it into your video editing software. When beginning to edit you may find the files are quite large and this can make the editing process slow. To solve this some video editing software allows the creation of "proxy" files. These are smaller versions of the same file that can be used during the edit and then, when it comes to exporting, the edits made on the proxy files are applied to the larger file at the point of export. If you do use such proxy features, make sure you know where all these temporary files are stored and anywhere that these files may be backed up. Many editors offer cloud storage by default so you may wish to disable this type of feature to prevent personal data being whisked away!

The next step is to place your video files onto the timeline. We recommend reviewing the footage and placing markers at all the places where personal data appears and disappears. When the markers have been placed you can then apply cuts to the content outside these markers. We also recommend leaving a one second gap between each remaining video clip, so the data subject is visually prompted that time has shifted in the footage. If a time stamp is not already imprinted into the footage one should be added to the start of each clip, so the user has this information. If you don't provide it, they will ask so it's worth pre-empting this follow-up.

After the cuts are made you will be left with only the footage you need. You can now begin the more technical aspects of the redaction process, editing within the footage itself. Most video editors have three tools that will help you semi-automate this redaction process. The first is the masking tool and this allows you to cut out areas within the footage, so they are no longer visible. In its basic form the masking tool is useful for masking objects that are static and remain in the same part of the footage throughout. The second tool is object tracking. Object tracking allows you to place a tracker on a particular object in a single frame of video. The software will track that object throughout all the frames the object is visible. This is useful for tracking the faces of third parties. The third tool is the blur or pixelate effect and this allows you to blur or pixelate an area of footage. The blur or pixelate feature can be used on its own, but it works best when combined with masks and object tracking to apply the effect dynamically throughout your footage.

The penultimate step is to process the audio. Where CCTV cameras pick up sound they may pick up confidential conversations off camera that are not related to the data subject. These will need to be removed. Similar steps can be followed as per the previous section about audio files but you need to be mindful when making cuts to audio that you don't inadvertently remove video at the same time. We recommend muting the section rather than cutting the audio. The final effect you may wish to apply to the footage is a visual watermark. A visual watermark can be overlayed on top of the footage with the details of the data subject. Applying a watermark can be particularly useful when the footage contains licenced material or where there is a risk of footage being re-edited and/or made public.

After applying the appropriate effects to redact the footage it is then time to export the file to a compatible file format. When it comes to exporting video file there are many common file formats and it can be quite confusing to the uninitiated. We recommend consulting the documentation of your video editor and conducting some test exports. A file that is around 12 megabytes per one minute of high-definition video will work on a laptop, tablet or mobile device. The video should open using the built-in video player. If you can't get the video to play it is highly unlikely your data subject will be able to get it to play either.

In terms of single images, a similar process to video applies. Masking and pixelation tools are common features of photo editing packages such as Photoshop (paid) and GIMP (free). We recommend saving the files in either JPEG (*.jpg) or PNG (*.png) file formats.

A question we often get, in addition to which file format to use, is what resolution should the footage/images be in? There is no perfect answer to this, but at a minimum, the resolution should be good enough for the data subject to view the material clearly. The material, however, does not need to be at a publishable resolution or suitable for a cinema screen. In most cases standard definition for video, 75dpi for images and 128bps for audio will usually suffice. The higher the resolution the higher the file size. If the material is to be transferred to a data subject using a physical drive large files may be less of a problem, but, if the files are to be transferred via the internet, large file sizes may be problematic for you to send, and for the data subject to receive. Now you have all your material redacted you are ready to produce the DSAR pack. .

# Produce

By this stage, a practitioner should have all the material requested by the data subject in one place. It should be in file formats that a data subject can open and will have been processed to remove material that the data subject is not entitled to see or hear. But it's not enough to simply send a batch of files to the data subject. Many pieces of data protection legislation, such as GDPR, require supplementary information to be included alongside the primary material. The reason for this is to aid the data subject in understanding what they have received. In this section we will work through how to put all this material together.

## The Primary Material

The primary DSAR material is a collection of the all the files that will go to the data subject. Generally, production of the primary material tends to fall into two camps, a physical product that may or may not contain digital material or a digital-only product. When making a DSAR under EU/UK law a data subject can request the material in digital or physical format. To our knowledge there is no legal requirement to make the material available over the internet. Therefore, if no preference has been made, controllers should consider the nature of the material and the delivery methods available to them – there will be more on delivery in the next chapter. As an extreme example, if the material requested is primarily CCTV footage it would not be appropriate to send the data subject a printout of every frame of video. It would, however, be appropriate to send the footage in the post, on physical media (securely encrypted of course!), if the file, or files, were too large to send by email or otherwise make available online.

Controllers may also wish to consider the method used to make the request. For example, if the data subject made a DSAR via email, it is more likely they would want the material provided in a digital format. The key thing is for the controller to confirm early in the DSAR process which format is desired by the data subject.

So, what should be included in the primary material? Taking the example of a digital only model we recommend creating a folder structure to house all the material. The top-level folder name should include the name, reference, and request date. Then create two lower folders labelled "primary material" and "supplementary material". The primary material folder will house the treated files to be provided to the data subject. Where possible, recommend adding the DSAR reference number to the metadata of each file and labelling each page of each document with the DSAR reference number too. Should this data ever end up on a hacking site, labelling will help confirm whether the underlying security breach occurred at the controller's end, or because of the data subject's equipment being compromised.

The final item to place in the folder is an index of the material. The index should include the name of the file, a brief description of the content and the hash of the file where appropriate. There are utilities that can be employed to semi-automate this index process or you can use the output of the hashing process described in the preserve section of chapter five.

It's worth noting the index file is not a mandatory requirement but it is very useful for the controller to include for several reasons. Firstly, it provides a checklist to confirm all the files have been included. Secondly, it acts as a tool to support any follow up questions made by the data subject, and thirdly, it can support any compliance related questions that may be made by a regulator should the data subject make a complaint.

When all the material has been added to the folder structure it is useful to open a sample set of the files to confirm they all open correctly

## Supplementary Information

As we alluded to at the beginning of this section, there is often a regulatory requirement to provide supplementary information to the data subject in addition to the primary material. In this section we will discuss the supplementary material required under EU/UK data protection legislation and also some additional supplementary material we recommend you provide to reduce the effort of follow-up enquiries. Depending on your jurisdiction, there may be different requirements to provide supplementary information (or you may be lucky and not have to provide any). It is therefore important to check what is required where you practice.

Before we walk through the material, you may recall in the last section, we created a primary material folder, we now recommend creating a "supplementary material" folder. In this folder we recommend placing the following documents:

**Copies of privacy notices**: In the EU/UK, the supplementary information listed in GDPR is also required to be included in a Controller's privacy notice. Rather than reinventing the wheel and producing another controlled document, include a copy of the privacy notice in PDF form in the supplementary material folder. In most cases, this will fulfil the minimum regulatory requirements as they relate to supplementary information. This, however, may not be universally true in all jurisdictions. If it isn't true for a certain jurisdiction by default, consider creating a privacy notice that also includes any supplementary information requirements and save yourself the effort of maintaining multiple documents. When including a copies of privacy notices, it's important to include all privacy notices that apply to the data subject. For example, a data subject may be subject to several privacy notices e.g., if they are an employee and a customer. If data is held in a third-party applications, you may also need to include these privacy notices too.

**Explanatory document**: Within the DSAR material there may be internal jargon, or abbreviations that may not be immediately obvious to a data subject. These should be explained. Additionally, where inferred data is derived from personal data, the inference process should also be explained. We recommend creating an explanatory document per data subject type (e.g. patient, customer, employee) that contains a glossary of terms found in the DSAR material, their definitions and, an explanation of how any inferred data was derived.

**Correspondence related to DSAR**: The final documents that we recommend placing in the DSAR folder are those relating to the data subject access request itself. This will include all the correspondence between the controller and the data subject. Keeping these separate, and in one place, will be helpful to demonstrate all the relevant steps to fulfil the DSAR have been made should a data subject challenge any aspect of the DSAR or make a complaint be made to the regulator.

It's worth pointing out, the content of the explanatory document is not the same as the supplementary material typically required by law, and it is not required to be provided, but it is material we have found data subjects frequently request. It's also worth pointing out that the DSAR correspondence doesn't need to be provided either. This correspondence occurred after the date the DSAR was made. However, by proactively including an explanatory document and the DSAR-related correspondence, controllers are less likely to get avoidable follow-up questions. If you receive a lot of DSARs, and a lot of follow-up question, this could significantly reduce the overall effort of your DSAR process.

# Reasonable Adjustments

We discussed the need to make reasonable adjustments for those with disabilities or specific needs in the last chapter. In terms of producing the material let's recap on adjustments controllers may wish to consider when providing material to a data subject who has accessibility needs.

- Supplying the DSAR material large print format
- Supplying the DSAR material in braille format
- If material is provided in electronic form:
  - ensuring the DSAR material is fully compatible with screen reading technology.
  - ensuring the DSAR material can be magnified, and that font size can be increased.
- Supplying supplementary material in audio format

This list is not exhaustive, but whichever methods you choose you need to ensure your processes incorporate steps to convert DSAR material into accessible formats. Some of the steps may require third party support (e.g., production of material in braille) and so consideration should be given as to how this will be done ahead of time. For example, have you identified appropriate suppliers and what are their lead times? Making reasonable adjustments should not delay the production of the DSAR material past the standard statutory deadline, and in certain jurisdictions may also be considered as unlawful.

# Clean-Up

As you complete the task of producing the DSAR material, you will find that you have a lot of excess material created at various stages of the DSAR process. You will have original raw files as a result of conducting searches. You will have unredacted copies of files and perhaps different versions of the same material in different file formats. You may also have files of files such as a mailbox export (*.pst) containing lots of individual email files. It's not uncommon to have more than 5 copies of the same data and much of it is in unredacted form and most likely contains lots of sensitive personal data. If you have backup policies on your folder system, there will also be a mirror copy - so potentially 10 or more copies of the data! All this excess DSAR material presents additional information security risk to both the controller and the data subject.

The more copies of data held, the more likely a copy could become compromised. As such, once the final pack has been produced, the material now needs to be cleaned up. With the exception of a single unredacted copy and the index files, we recommend securely deleting all the other material on the day the DSAR is sent to the data subject. We then recommend retaining the unredacted copy for nine months. We then retaining the index files and a log of the request for the time period related to a statute of limitations for data protection offences. For example, in the UK this is currently six years but could be shorter or longer in your jurisdiction. If possible, consider implementing retention policies on the relevant folders so that files are automatically deleted at each point. If a complaint is made then a litigation hold policy should be applied to the material until the complaint is resolved.

The reason for holding the single unredacted copy for a longer period than the rest of the material is to support any follow-up questions from the data subjects and to support any investigation should the data subject make a complaint to a regulator. A data subject may take months to make a complaint and then a regulator may take several months before initiating an investigation. Remember more than half of all complaints to the UK data protection regulator were linked to the right of access and there are a lot of complaints. The likelihood of a complaint is therefore quite high. Hopefully, though, if you have followed our advice complaints should be less likely for you!

# Summary

The focus of this chapter was to work through the treatment phases of the Right to Access Fulfilment Model. Firstly, we looked at the review phase. We considered the need to reduce and deduplicate the output of searches to minimise effort later. We considered the need to find material that identified third parties, was covered by exemptions or contained intellectual property to allow such material to be removed as necessary. We then discussed when it may be appropriate to seek legal advice.

Secondly, we took a deep dive into redaction. We discussed why redaction is important to ensure the material provided contains only material related to the data subject. We walked through the redaction processes for text-based material, and for audio and visual file formats. We then offered some additional tips to consider when redacting documents that should make your life easier.

Finally, we considered the production element. We discussed the need to augment the primary material with supplementary information, so the data subject understands the material they have been provided. In the closing section we recapped the need to make reasonable adjustments to ensure the DSAR material is accessible to data subjects with accessibility needs.

Now we have treated the DSAR material it's now time to move on to the final stage of the RAFM – the delivery phase.

# Chapter Eight – Delivery Phase

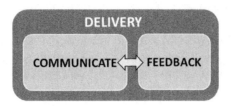

*Figure 14 - Delivery Phase*

There should be no doubting when you are dealing with DSARs you will inevitably need to keep in contact with the data subject throughout the process. Even when the DSAR material has been provided the data subject may have several follow-up questions, or may wish to exercise another one, or more, of their data protection rights. In more challenging DSARs there may be complaints to deal with, and in extreme situations there may be a need to communicate with a Data Protection Regulator. If you are dealing with several, or possibly hundreds (or thousands) of DSARs in parallel, it is going to be imperative you have a way of communicating effectively with the data subject in the first instance, and also a way to provide feedback to relevant stakeholders as needed. This is where the delivery phase of the RAFM comes in to its own!

Like the Preparation phase, there are two sub-components of the RAFM delivery phase - **Communicate** and **Feedback**. In the communicate section we will look at the pipeline of likely communication that may occur between a controller and a data subject. We will walk through some template letters that practitioners may wish to consider when formulating their own custom DSAR responses. We will also briefly discuss a few of the common outcomes that may follow after the completion of a DSAR such as further rights requests, complaints, or potential regulatory involvement.

In the feedback section we will look at how the DSAR process feeds back into the wider Data Protection regime within the organisation. DSARs often throw up seemingly unrelated data protection issues and it's important these issues are appropriately captured and tracked.

And, if you get through this chapter in one piece, you will have worked through every phase of the Right to Access Fulfilment Model. But we're not there just yet!  So, let's get started with this final chapter…

# Communication

In the communication section we will do a deep dive into the communication component of the Right to Access Fulfilment Model. Communicating effectively with the data subject could mean the difference between a straightforward DSAR and a nightmare ending in litigation and regulatory enforcement so it's important to get it right! With that in mind there are two things to think about. Firstly we will discuss security. More specifically, how to securely transfer the material to the data subject. Secondly, we will discuss the key components to effective communication management and how to communicate effectively with data subjects. We will then conclude the section with by walking through the various templates a controller may wish to produce to ensure communication with the data subject is managed and items are not overlooked. Ok, lets crack on!

## Security in Transit

A DSAR is highly likely to contain sensitive material about the data subject and their relationship with the controller. As we have highlighted in the examples throughout the book DSAR material could contain references to employment issues, medical issues, or safeguarding issues. Any sensitive material inadvertently disclosed to a third party could present a high risk to the data subject involved. As such, the material must be securely transferred from the controller to the data subject. There are several ways to do this which we will now discuss. The first consideration will be whether the material is to be transferred in physical form or transferred electronically. Let's look at each in turn:

**Physical form**: Physical form could be a file of paper documents or files stored on a physical storage medium (e.g. USB drive or a DVD). Any digital files should be encrypted on the storage medium in such a manner that they can be opened on the data subject's device. A common method is to place the files in an encrypted zip file and then send the password by email or SMS or a separate letter. The material should be placed in an envelope which is then placed in another envelope. This double enveloping prevents accidental compromise should the outer envelope become damaged. The package should then be sent by a trusted postal service whereby the data subject must sign for and accept delivery. Controllers should then keep a record of the postal transfer and have follow-up processes in place should the package not be delivered.

On rare occasions a data subject may refuse to sign for the DSAR material as they think they are entering into some form of contract to agree the material is complete. If you feel this may be an issue, it is worth pre-empting this by letting the data subject know ahead of time that they are only confirming receipt of the material and that confirming receipt does not impact on their ability to further exercise their data protection rights.

**Digital Only Form**: Generally there are three types of mechanism to transfer files to data subjects is a digital only form that could be considered reasonably secure. The first is a secure portal where the data subject must login to access the material This portal could be built into an existing application, be a standalone application or, it could be a service hosted by a third party such as an electronic data room. Whichever option is used, the controller must ensure that the portal is secure from unauthorised access and where a third party service is involved that a processing agreement is in place.

The second is to send via secure email. Secure email could be as basic as using enforced TLS or it could be a secure email portal. Secure email portals are preferred by some organisations as it keeps all the email correspondence within the portal which mitigates the possibility of material becoming compromised should someone inadvertently send an email to the incorrect recipient.

The third is to transfer the file using a file drop system. File drops systems are not inherently secure and are not recommended if other methods are available but may be appropriate for large files where the compromise of content would be low risk to the data subject. File drop services should only be used where there is a processor agreement in place i.e. do not use free services. This method requires the controller to first encrypt the material using a strong encryption algorithm and applying a complex password of at least 15 characters. The material is then uploaded to the file drop location. The data subject is then sent a time-limited link to access the material by email. The password should then be sent by post or SMS.

As you can see there are several different methods, and no one size fits all. Controllers must decide which option works for their particular set of circumstances. It may also be the case that more than one method is used depending on the nature request and the needs of the data subject.

OK, now we know how to communicate securely, lets now look at how to communicate effectively!

## Communication Management

Effective management of communication is essential when dealing with Data Subject Access Requests. As we now know, DSARs are the most frequently used data protection right, and controllers must ensure their communication with the data subject is effectively managed. In this section we will explore some critical factors to consider when managing communication in the context of DSARs.

Firstly, it's essential to have clear and effective communication with the individual making the request, as well as with any internal stakeholders involved in providing the requested information. This can include IT, legal, and customer service teams among others. Secondly, when communicating with the individual making the request, it's important to be transparent about the information you hold, how it's processed, and the rights the individual has in relation to that data. This will help build trust and ensure the individual's expectations are managed throughout the process.

Thirdly, internal communication is crucial in managing DSARs. It's important to have clear processes in place for managing requests, including who is responsible for each step of each process, how information is collected and reviewed, and how any necessary redactions or exemptions are identified and applied. We have covered each of these activities in detail throughout the book, and the person responsible for the DSAR process will need to decide who will fulfil each activity …and communicate this to the relevant parties!

By having a clear and effective process in place for managing DSARs, including a focus on communication management, organisations can ensure they comply with data protection laws and build trust with individuals whose personal data they hold.

## Template Preparation

Whilst there will always be unique DSAR scenarios one DSAR made to your organisation is likely to be very similar to the next. It should, therefore, make sense to create a template for each type of communication. By creating communication templates every time a DSAR comes in the correct communication can be provided consistently without having to create everything from scratch. In addition, if someone new joins the team they won't have to start from nothing, they can simply fill in the core details and issue to the data subject with little supervision. Surprisingly, many organisations don't use templated responses and end up spending significant amounts of time providing unique responses to each DSAR. This not only wastes time but can also lead to key pieces of information being omitted from the communication, e.g., the right by the data subject to make a complaint to the data protection regulator. It can't be restated enough that good communication can be the difference between a data subject walking away happy with your initial response or a disgruntled data subject escalating the issue to your data protection regulator. So, what should we have in our DSAR template library? It's useful to split up your templates into four stages:

- Stage 1 – Preamble
- Stage 2 – Response
- Stage 3 – Follow Up
- Stage 4 – Complaints

Let's discuss the communication a controller may need to provide to the data subject at each of these stages.

## But first ... Reasonable Adjustments

Hopefully you will recall we discussed the need to make reasonable adjustments for those with disabilities or specific needs in a previous chapter. If you're planning on using the example templates in this book, and prior to issuing any communication, please consider your data subjects needs and the requirements of your local equalities' legislation.

## Preamble

In the preamble stage the primary objective is to ensure we have enough information from the data subject to minimise the amount of data we need to process and, more importantly, ensure we have a valid DSAR from a verified data subject! The following communications should be considered as part of the preamble stage:

**Acknowledgement**: An acknowledgement should be sent to the data subject as soon as possible on receipt of the request and ideally within 48hours.

Remember, DSARs can come from many different channels and could be made to any member of staff, or a staff member at one of your processors, and as we also know, DSARs may not necessarily be labelled as a DSAR either. Remember, _everyone_ needs to know how to identify a DSAR and the process to follow to acknowledge the data subject has made such a request. The ideal process would be for a request to be forwarded to a central case management tool which would then send out this initial acknowledgement automatically.

Although less ideal, another approach could be to forward the DSARs to a DSAR mailbox that is monitored by the person responsible for data protection in your organisation. Alternatively, it could be those most likely to encounter a data subject, e.g., Customer Service Representatives, are trained to carry out the initial acknowledgement. The key point is that whoever initially receives the request needs to set in motion a process to acknowledge the DSAR. Acknowledgements don't need to be lengthy, and the following template gives an example of a suitable response.

---

Dear **[Name]**,

**Data Subject Access Request – [Reference]**

Thank you for your **[Insert Correspondence Type]**. Your DSAR reference is **[Reference]**.

We confirm we have received your Data Subject Access Request made on **[Insert**

---

**Date]**. We will review your request and come back to you within two working days if we have any follow up questions or need to verify your identity. If you don't hear from us within two working days we will process your DSAR and aim to have the requested material with you no later than **[Insert Date]**.

In rare circumstances a DSAR may be considered complex. We will aim to let know you if your DSAR is determined as complex within seven working days and will provide an explanation and the estimated additional time we may need to supply the material to you.

In the meantime, as a caring organisation we wish to ensure we consider any individual requirements you may have with regard to receiving the information we hold. If you have any specific needs, for example providing the material in large print or braille, please let us know so we can make reasonable adjustments to our standard process. We have contacted you using the same medium in which you have made your request, if you would like to discuss your needs using a different medium please let us know.

If you have any questions, please don't hesitate to get in touch, quoting your DSAR reference on **[insert contact details]**.

Yours sincerely,

**[Signature Block]**

*Figure 15 - Acknowledgment Letter*

**Confirming Identity**: In certain circumstances you may need to verify the data subject's identity before proceeding with a Data Subject Access Request. Requesting identification should not be made in the initial acknowledgement communication as in some cases the identity of the data subject is already known. It should be obvious that asking someone with whom you are currently discussing a sensitive matter with to verify their identity is likely to make your organisation look inept and further inflame an already difficult situation. Take care to only verify identification where the identity of the requestor is not already confirmed.

Dear **[Name]**,

**Data Subject Access Request – Identification Check Required – [Reference]**

On **[Insert Date]** you made a Data Subject Access Request. In order to ensure the personal data our organisation holds is supplied to the correct person we need to carry out some checks to verify your identity.

**[Where the identity verification process involves processing identity documents, we will retain the documents for {Insert Retention Period}.]**

We would therefore ask you to provide the following information:

[Fully Describe Method One] OR [Fully Describe Method Two] *
*Where possible give the data subject more than one mechanism.

Please note we will not begin to process your Data Subject Access Request until we have verified your identity.

If we do not receive a response to this identity verification check we will send a reminder after eight working days. If there is no response we will close the request without further action after ten working days. You can respond after this period, if doing so please provide your Data Subject Access Request reference and we will reopen and restart your request.

Yours sincerely,

**[Signature Block]**

*Figure 16 - Identification Request Letter*

In some cases, you may be provided with incorrect identity information. In these situations it is useful to communicate this to the data subject as soon as possible so they are aware of the issue and can return with a corrected response.

Dear **[Name]**,

**Data Subject Access Request – Unable to Verify Identification – [Reference]**

We have been unable to verify your identity based on the information you provided.

The reason for this is because **[insert reason(s)]**. If you are able to provide corrected information, we will review this on receipt.

Please note we will not begin to process your Data Subject Access Request until we have verified your identity.

If we have not received a response within five working days, we will close the request without further action. You can respond after this period, if doing so please provide your Data Subject Access Request reference and we will reopen and restart the request.

Yours sincerely,

**[Signature Block]**

*Figure 17 - Unable to Verify Identification Letter*

If the identity check has been completed successfully it is good practice is to let the data subject know. If there is no need to clarify the DSAR requirements the following response could be used:

---

Dear **[Name]**,

**Data Subject Access Request – Identification Verified – [Reference]**

Thank you for providing the requested information. We have now verified your identity and will commence the processing of the Data Subject Access Request.

At this stage we have everything we need to fulfil your request. If we need to seek any clarification or apply an extension, we will contact you as soon as possible to let you know.

*[As the identity verification process involved processing identity documents, we shall retain the documents for **{Insert Retention Period}**.]*

Yours sincerely,

**[Signature Block]**

---

*Figure 18 - Identification Verified Letter*

From time to time DSARs may originate from a third party, e.g., a Solicitor. In such cases, and to avoid inadvertently providing data to someone without authority, you may want to verify with the data subject that the third party does have authority to make the DSAR on their behalf.

---

Dear **[Name]**,

**Data Subject Access Request – Verification of Third Party Authority – [Reference]**

A Data Subject Access Request has been made on your behalf by the third party listed below on **[Insert Date]**.

**[Insert details of third-party requestor]**

The third party provided the following reference **[Insert Reference]** and a copy of the request has been included as an attachment/enclosure to this communication.

In order to ensure we don't disclose your Personal Data to this third party without your authority please respond to this communication confirming this third party is authorised to act upon your behalf. If we do not hear from you within the next seven working days we will act on the basis that you have not authorised the request and will consider the matter closed.

If you have any questions relating to this matter, please do not hesitate to get in contact.

Yours sincerely,

**[Signature Block]**

*Figure 19 - Verifying Third Party Authority*

At the end of the seven-day period, if the data subject has not authorised the third party request, you may wish to communicate with the third party to let them know. They can chase this up with the data subject if the request was valid.

Dear **[Name]**,

**Data Subject Access Request – Authority not provided by data subject – [Reference]**

A Data Subject Access Request was made on behalf of **[Insert data subject name]** by the third party listed below on **[Insert Date]**.

**[Insert details of third-party requestor]**

In order to ensure we don't disclose Personal Data to a third party without authorisation we requested authority to act directly from the data subject on **[Insert Date]**. The data subject did not respond within the subsequent seven working day response period. We have therefore taken this to mean you are not authorised to make the request and now consider the matter closed.

If you do have authority to act, we recommend you contact the data subject to understand why they declined to respond to our prior correspondence.

Yours sincerely,

**[Signature Block]**

*Figure 20 - Declining Third Party Request*

**Clarification**: When you have confidence you are talking to the correct data subject you may wish to clarify the nature of the DSAR. Remember, when the identification of the data subject has been verified the clock is ticking on providing a response. If you are going to clarify do it as soon as possible and keep the deadline for a response short. You don't want to be waiting a week to be then told they want everything anyway and you now have one week less to pull everything together. An example of a clarification letter is below:

147

Dear **[Name]**,

**Data Subject Access Request – Clarification – [Reference]**

We would like to clarify the nature of your/the data subject access request and in doing so would ask for the following information: -

- The date range of your request (e.g., material between May and June)

- Any keywords you would like us to search against (e.g., if you have used a nickname)

- If you are seeking data on a particular topic (e.g., material related to my redundancy)

- **[Anything else you would like to clarify]**

We want to let you know you are not required to narrow down the DSAR but in doing so we may be able to supply you with the material more quickly and may also reduce the possibility we need to apply an extension to your request.

If we don't hear from you within three working days, we will work on the premise you require everything we hold. If your request is determined to be a complex case, we will inform you as soon as possible if we require an extension. If we don't require additional time the current date, we aim to provide you with the DSAR material is no later than **[Insert Date]**.

Yours sincerely,

**[Signature Block]**

*Figure 21 - Clarification Letter*

**Extensions**: In some cases, and where the local legislation permits e.g., where there is complexity, you may need to inform the data subject you will be applying an extension. Where this is the case you need to tell the data subject as soon as possible and no later than the statutory deadline. A good rule of thumb would be within two weeks of the original request. This should give you sufficient time to have carried out the initial searches and assessed the amount of processing that will be required. Don't leave it to the date of the deadline as that pretty much tells the data subject the extension is more a stalling technique than a genuine requirement. Whatever timeframe you choose, ensure you let the data subject know ***before*** the initial statutory deadline (in the UK this is 30 days). If you do not meet this deadline there is a high chance the data subject will escalate the issue to their data protection regulator as a complaint. If it is a complex case you really don't want to be dealing with a regulator too! The following letter is an example of how the application of an extension can be communicated to the data subject:

Dear **[Name]**,

**Data Subject Access Request – Extension Required – [Reference]**

You submitted the above referenced subject access request on **[Insert Date]**. Upon review we have identified some complexity which means we need to invoke an extension. The reason for this is:

*[ - We have experienced technical difficulties in retrieving your personal data from our systems and this has slowed down our ability to process your request.*

*- We need to apply an exemption that involves large volumes of particularly sensitive information.*

*- As you are a third party, we are still trying to clarify confidentiality issues around the disclosure of sensitive medical information relating to the data subject.*

*- Due to the complex nature of your request, we have needed to obtain specialist legal advice.*

*- Your request involves searching large volumes of unstructured manual records (only applicable to public authorities).]* ***[\*Delete/Modify/Add to these examples as appropriate]***

As a result of these complexities the deadline for providing you with the material requested will now be no later than **[Insert Date]**. Whilst this is the current deadline we will do our utmost to get the material to you as quickly as possible.

Yours sincerely,

**[Signature Block]**

*Figure 22 - Extension Letter*

**Third Party Information**: It is possible a data subject may ask for information that relates to a third party which is covered by an applicable exemption, for example the content of a confidential reference. In cases where an exemption exists and information does not need to be provided, a controller may wish to make reasonable enquiries to the third party to establish whether they would be willing to allow the disclosure of the exempted information to the data subject, and in doing so override the exemption from disclosure. In order to avoid any confusion as to whether disclosure was permitted it is useful to seek the written permission of the third party.

Dear **[Name]**,

**Data Subject Access Request – Authority to provide your Personal Data to a Third Party – [Reference]**

We have received a Data Subject Access Request from **[insert data subject name]**. In the course of this request, they have specifically asked for information to which we owe you a duty of confidence. The information is as follows:

**[Insert details of the information requested]**

Copies of the information detailed above are attached/enclosed.

Would you be willing to authorise the disclosure of this information? Please let us know your decision in writing within seven working days of this request. If you do not respond within seven working days, we will conclude you have not provided authority for disclosure.

Please note the data subject may challenge any decision we make in applying exemptions and may escalate a complaint to the Data Protection Regulator. If we are compelled to provide this data by the Data Protection Regulator, we will advise you as to what has been provided in accordance with your data protection rights.

Yours sincerely,

**[Signature Block]**

*Figure 23 - Authority to provide Personal Data to a Third Party*

The above set of correspondence should cover most of the scenarios a controller may face during the pre-amble stage of communication with the data subject, however this is not exhaustive. You may also wish to consider your own sector or organisational needs and any acknowledgements related to interactions with third parties. For example, if you are in an educational or medical setting you may wish to draft templates related to competence. You may also wish to draft correspondence to clarify whether the request is a DSAR or whether the requestor is exercising the rights of access afforded by other legislation e.g., Education (Pupil Information) (England) Regulations or Access to Health Care Records Act.

# Response

The response stage contains the most common communications you might send to a data subject after you have assessed the request and determined what, if any, information you are obligated to provide under your local data protection legislation, .

A DSAR response will generally fall into one of five categories. They are:

- The data subject is entitled to all the information you hold
- The data subject is entitled to some of the information you hold
- There is no data held relating to the data subject
- The data held on the data subject has not changed since their last request
- The data subject's request is manifestly unfounded or excessive

**Base Response**: Let's have a look at examples of each. First up, the base response. This is where the data subject is entitled to all the information you hold. The base response must include how to access and navigate the DSAR material, how to exercise any other data protection rights, e.g., the right to rectification, and, how to make a complaint, including a making a complaint to the data protection regulator.

---

Dear **[Name]**,

**Data Subject Access Request – Response – [Reference]**

You made a Data Subject Access Request on **[Insert Date]** and we are pleased to provide you with the requested information within the statutory deadline. The information is *[attached in a password protected file/available at the following link/contained on the included physical storage device in a password protected file/contained (at your request) in physical form]* *__[Delete/Modify as appropriate]__*

For security reasons the password to open the files has been sent to you via **[insert method used to communicate the password]**. If you have not received the password, please let us know.

In addition to the information itself, and to help you navigate the material, we have included a glossary of terms and an index of the files with a description of the personal data they contain. We hope you find this useful but if you have any questions, please do let us know. The DSAR material provided will be retained for **[insert retention period]** before being securely destroyed. Details of your request, but not the material, will be retained for six years. If the material provided is inaccurate and you would like us to correct our records, or if you have any other queries about how we use your data, please let us know. Your information is processed as laid down in our Privacy Notice **[Insert Link]**.

The information provided may contain material covered under Intellectual Property Law. Copyright material must not be copied, distributed, modified, reproduced, transmitted, published (including published on the Internet or an intranet), or otherwise made available in whole or in part without the prior written consent of the copyright holder. If you wish to perform any of the actions listed above, please contact us for further guidance.

---

We hope you are happy with the response.  Please let us know if you have any concerns so we may attempt to address them. If you are not happy with our response you can make a complaint to the Data Protection Regulator.  You can find further information here on their website [insert information for relevant Data Protection Regulator]

Yours sincerely,

**[Signature Block]**

*Figure 24 - DSAR Base Response*

**No Data Held:** The next response is where there is no data held by the controller. This scenario could occur where a data subject has previously had a relationship with the controller, but retention periods related to the data subject's personal data have lapsed and therefore the personal data has been destroyed. It may be the data subject is aware of your retention periods and wants to confirm their data has been destroyed. The following template is an example of a response where no data is held:

Dear **[Name]**,

**Data Subject Access Request – Response – [Reference]**

You made a Data Subject Access Request on **[Insert Date]** and we are pleased to provide you with a response within the statutory deadline. After conducting searches within our systems and those of our processors we can confirm that we do not currently hold any of your personal data.

We hope you are happy with this response.  Please let us know if you have any concerns so we may attempt to address them.  If you are not happy with our response you can make a complaint to the Data Protection Regulator. You can find further information here on their website [insert information for relevant Data Protection Regulator]

Yours sincerely,

**[Signature Block]**

*Figure 25 - DSAR Response Where No Data Held*

**Exemptions Applied**: The exemptions applied response is similar to the base response but includes details of which exemptions have been applied to the DSAR or a description of the information that has been provided instead of the original material. A common scenario where exemption and descriptions are applied is where the data subject is making a DSAR to their employer.

Dear **[Name]**,

**Data Subject Access Request – Response – [Reference]**

You made a Data Subject Access Request on the **[Insert Date]** and we are pleased to provide you with the requested information within the statutory deadline. The information is *[attached in a password protected file/available at the following link/contained on the included physical storage device in a password protected file/contained (at your request) in physical form]* *[Delete/Modify as appropriate]*

For security reasons the password to open the files has been sent to you via **[insert method used to communicate the password]**. If you have not received the password, please let us know.

As an employee your personal data was included in a significant volume of emails, instant messages and digital files relating to your role as **[insert role]**. With exception to those that relate directly to you as a data subject this material has not been included in the DSAR response due to its confidential nature. Additionally, and where applicable under data protection law, some material has been redacted.

In the case of your DSAR the following exemptions have been applied:

Legal Professional Privilege. This exemption relates to where we have sought legal advice relating to the information you have requested.

Management Information. This exemption relates to information relating to ongoing organisational restructuring activities.

Negotiations with the Requestor. This exemption relates to information regarding our ongoing negotiations with you relating to your exit from the organisation.

Confidential References. This exemption relates to references provided by third parties to whom we owe a duty of confidence.

Further information on the exemptions we have applied can be found here: [Insert link to exemption information from relevant data protection regulator].

In addition to the information itself, and to help you navigate the material, we have included a glossary of terms and an index of the files with a description of the personal data they contain. We hope you find this useful but if you have any questions, please do let us know. The DSAR material provided will be retained for **[insert retention period]** and then securely destroyed. Details of your request, but not the material, will be retained for six years. If the material provided is inaccurate and you would like us to correct our records, or if you have any other queries about how we use your data, please let us know.

Your information is processed as laid down in our Privacy Notice **[Insert Link]**.

The information provided may contain material covered under Intellectual Property Law. Copyright material must not be copied, distributed, modified, reproduced, transmitted, published (including published on the Internet or an intranet), or otherwise made available in whole or in part without the prior written consent of the copyright holder. If you wish to perform any of the actions listed above, please contact us for further guidance.

We hope you are happy with this response. Please let us know if you have any concerns so we may attempt to address them. If you are not happy with our response you can make a complaint to the Data Protection Regulator. You can find further information on their website [insert information for relevant Data Protection Regulator]

Yours sincerely,

**[Signature Block]**

*Figure 26 - DSAR Response Where Exemptions have been applied.*

**No change in Personal Data**:  There may be occasions where a data subject makes more than one DSAR in a short period of time. Unless the data subject's request is manifestly unfounded or excessive there is nothing that prevents a data subject from making more than one DSAR. If you have already provided the material to the data subject, you are not obliged to keep providing the same material over and over again. If nothing has changed you can simply communicate this fact to the data subject. Similarly, if a data subject makes a request shortly after you have responded to a previous DSAR it is reasonable to provide only the material that has been created or updated since the last request. That is to say any new searches would be limited from the date of the previous searches. Figure 27 is an example of such a response.

Dear **[Name]**,

**Data Subject Access Request – Response – [Reference]**

You made a **[second]** Data Subject Access Request on **[Insert Date]** and we are pleased to provide you with the requested information within the statutory deadline. The information is *[attached in a password protected file/available at the following link/contained on the included physical storage device in a password protected file/contained (at your request) in physical form] \*[Delete/Modify as appropriate]*

For security reasons the password to open the files has been sent to you via **[insert communication method used to send password]**. If you have not received the password please let us know.

As your previous Data Subject Access Request was made on **[Insert Date]** the material provided within this response contains only material created or updated since this date. Additionally, and where applicable under data protection law, some material has been redacted within this current request. In the case of this DSAR the following exemptions have been applied:

Legal Professional Privilege. This exemption relates to where we have sought legal advice relating to the information you have requested.

Negotiations with the Requestor. This exemption relates to information regarding our ongoing negotiations with you relating to your exit from the organisation.

Management Information. This exemption relates to information relating to ongoing organisational restructuring activities.

Confidential References. This exemption relates to references provided by third parties to whom we owe a duty of confidence.

Further information on the exemptions we have applied can be found here: [Insert link to exemption information from relevant data protection regulator].

In addition to the information itself, and to help you navigate the material, we have included a glossary of terms and an index of the files with a description of the personal data they contain. We hope you find this useful but if you have any questions, please do let us know. The DSAR material provided will be retained for **[insert retention period]** and then securely destroyed. Details of your request, but not the material, will be retained for six years. If the material provided is inaccurate and you would like us to correct our records or, if you have any other queries about how we use your data, please let us know. Your information is processed as laid down in our Privacy Notice **[Insert Link]**.

The information provided may contain material covered under Intellectual Property Law. Copyright material must not be copied, distributed, modified, reproduced, transmitted, published (including published on the Internet or an intranet), or otherwise made available in whole or in part without the prior written consent of the copyright holder. If you wish to perform any of the actions listed above, please contact us for further guidance.

We hope you are happy with this response. Please let us know if you have any concerns so we may attempt to address them. If you are not happy with our response you can make a complaint to the Data Protection Regulator. You can find further information on their website [insert information for relevant Data Protection Regulator].

Yours sincerely,

**[Signature Block]**

*Figure 27 - Response to Additional DSAR*

**Manifestly Excessive/Unfounded DSAR**: There could be times when you will need to respond to a manifestly unfounded or excessive DSAR. In such circumstances you may wish to inform the data subject you will not be providing the information requested. If you are choosing not to comply with such a request, you need to make sure that your response includes the following:

- Confirmation that you do hold the data subject's personal data
- That the request has been assessed and deemed to be either manifestly unfounded and/or excessive
- Valid reasons to support your assessment (i.e., not that you have a manifestly excessive retention schedule and don't want to trawl through tens of thousands of emails you should have already deleted!)
- The data subject's right to make a complaint to the Data Protection Regulator
- The data subject's right to seek judicial remedy

In figure 28 is an example of a response a controller might make to a manifestly unfounded DSAR:

Dear **[Name]**,

**Data Subject Access Request – Response – [Reference]**

You made a Data Subject Access Request on **[Insert Date]**. We have reviewed the content of your request and have determined the request is manifestly unfounded for the reasons stated below:

**[Insert reason the request is determined as manifestly unfounded e.g., You offered to withdraw your request if we pay you the sum of £1750].**

As a result of determining the request manifestly unfounded we will not be processing your Data Subject Access Request.

We would also like to advise you that you can make a complaint to the Data Protection Regulator should you not be happy with our response. You can find further information here on their website [insert information for relevant Data Protection Regulator].

You may also wish to know that, in addition to your right to make a complaint to the Data Protection Regulator, you also have the right to seek a judicial remedy through the courts.

| Yours sincerely, |
| --- |
| **[Signature Block]** |

Figure 28 - Manifestly Unfounded DSAR Response

The above set of correspondence should cover most of the scenarios that a controller may face during the response stage of communication with the data subject. As with the pre-amble stage you may also wish to consider your own sectoral or organisational needs.

## Follow-Up

In most cases when the DSAR material has been provided to the data subject that is the end of the process. That said, we don't want to give you false hope. This may not be the case for your organisation as many factors shape how a data subject reacts to the material you have provided to them.

In this section we will look at some of the more common issues that arise post DSAR submission. They are:

- The data subject believes that material is missing
- The data subject believes material has been excessively redacted
- The data subject has been maligned by a third party wishes to know the identity of that person, or persons',
- The data subject wishes to exercise other data protection rights

In each of the above situations there will be scenarios where the data subject is correct in their assessment and there will be situations where they may not. For example, there will be situations where the data subject can exercise their rights under data protection legislation, and in others, subject to the lawful basis of the underlying processing activity, those rights may be constrained.

**Data missing from original request**: Even if you have performed an exhaustive search of keywords relating to a data subject with a highly unique name, so it's highly unlikely you have missed anything, the data subject could still believe material is missing. Let's look at an example of a uniquely named data subject named Charles Xavier van deGrasse-Tyson who has recently received his completed DSAR material. Charles is adamant that something is missing and has written back with words to the effect that the DSAR is incomplete. Unfortunately, in doing so he doesn't tell you what he believes is missing in the first instance. Upon sending a clarification email to ascertain what material Charles believes is missing he provides a further identifier "MrX2023" - his username for an online service your organisation's subsidiary provides. When conducting searches on this username additional material is identified. Figure 29 describes a potential response.

Dear **[Name]**,

**Data Subject Access Request – [Reference] – Follow up to your enquiry**

Further to your post-DSAR enquiry dated **[insert date]**, we can confirm that, when using the new search terms, additional information has been identified on our systems. This material was excluded in error, and we apologise that this material was not included in the original request. We will process the newly identified material and send it to you by **[insert date]**. We have also investigated the root cause of the error and are updating our DSAR process to minimise such an omission reoccurring.

We hope you accept our apology but would like to let you know that you can make a complaint to the Data Protection Regulator should you wish to do so. You can find further information here on their website [insert information for relevant Data Protection Regulator].

Yours sincerely,

**[Signature Block]**

*Figure 29 - DSAR Follow Up - Additional Material Identified*

When you have processed the material, it is recommended you send out an appropriate communication from the response section ensuring the new response reflects any exemptions applied to the new material. If no further material is found during additional searches a response such as the one in Figure 30 could be used. Figures 29 and 30 could also be modified to provide appropriate responses where material has been excessively redacted.

Dear **[Name]**,

**Data Subject Access Request – [Reference] – Follow up to your enquiry.**

Further to your post-DSAR enquiry dated **[insert date]**, we can confirm after conducting additional searches within our systems and those of our processors, that we do not hold any additional personal data in addition to the material provided on **[insert date]**.

We hope you are happy with this response.  Please let us know if you have any concerns so we may attempt to address them.  If you are not happy with our response you can make a complaint to the Data Protection Regulator.

You can find further information on their website [insert information for relevant Data Protection Regulator].

Yours sincerely,

**[Signature Block]**

*Figure 30 - DSAR Follow Up - No Material Identified*

**Request for material relating to a Third Party**: Sadly, there are many occasions where material in a DSAR contains hurtful comments relating to the data subject and they may wish to know who made the comments. As a couple of examples, the data subject might be a customer and a call centre representative could have written in an email that the data subject is a horrible person. The data subject might be an employee and a colleague has written in an IM that they are incompetent or have poor personal hygiene. On other occasions the data subject may be part of a selection process, e.g., for a new role or perhaps during a redundancy process and want to know how they scored against others. Whilst the data subject may wish to know what has been said about them, the controller also has a duty to protect the personal data of third parties just as much as that of the data subject.

Where third party information is requested, unless the third party has given permission for their information to be disclosed or a controller is legally compelled to provide third party identity information, the request should be politely denied as per figure 31.

---

Dear **[Name]**,

**Data Subject Access Request – [Reference] – Follow up to your enquiry.**

Further to your post-DSAR enquiry dated **[insert date]** requesting **[state requested information, e.g., the identities and score breakdowns of the third parties that were also involved in the recent redundancy process]**. We will not be providing this information **[state reason the information will not be provided, e.g., as this falls outside the scope of your right to access in so far as the material requested does not relate to you]**. [In addition to the material falling out of scope of your data protection rights *delete as appropriate] We also have a duty of confidence to all those involved in the process.in the same way we have a duty of confidence to you not to provide your personal data to a third party without a lawful basis.

We understand you may not be happy with this response. We would like to let you know that whilst this is our final position you can make a complaint to the Data Protection Regulator should you wish to do so.

You can find further information on their website [insert information for relevant Data Protection Regulator].

---

| Yours sincerely,

**[Signature Block]** |

Figure 31 - DSAR Follow Up - Denying request for Third Party Data

**Exercising other rights**: Another common follow-up to a DSAR is for the data subject to exercise a further data protection right based on the information they have identified in the DSAR material. This could be engaging their right to rectification should the DSAR material reveal inaccuracies, or another example could be exercising their right to be forgotten. This might be because they have identified material, they no longer wish a controller to hold. A good example of this could be where an ex-employee requests that emails of a personal nature stored in their old corporate account are deleted. Finally, the data subject may see processing they didn't expect to and may wish to exercise their right to object. An example of this could be where the data subject wasn't aware a controller was inferring data points based on their online activity. In cases where another right is being engaged the DSAR process has technically concluded, therefore it's useful to reset communication to reference the other new right(s) request. An example of a reset communication template that could be used when the right to rectification is being exercised is in figure 32.

| Dear **[Name]**,

**Right to Rectification Request – [Reference] - Address Correction**

Thank you for contacting us on **[insert date]** to let us know that upon reviewing the material in your Data Subject Access Request you found the personal data we hold about you to be inaccurate. Specifically, that the **[insert incorrect information]** we hold in our records is incorrect.

As you have already provided supplementary evidence in the form **[insert evidence that has been provided]** I have now passed this on to the relevant team who will update your record with the correct information. This should be updated within **[insert timeframe.**

In the meantime, if you have any further questions please don't hesitate to get in touch.

Yours sincerely,

**[Signature Block]** |

Figure 32 - DSAR Follow-Up – Different Data Protection Right Request

By following this structure and resetting the process you have created for managing other data protection rights it is less likely that a controller will lose track of each request. Managing rights requests individually will also mean you can generate meaningful metrics about how well each process is doing – so it's a win-win!

## Complaints

Now this is not a book on complaints management – there are plenty of other books that cover this topic – but there will be times where a DSAR results in a complaint so it's useful to briefly discuss how complaints specifically related to the DSAR process could be handled. This section is not covering all types of complaints just those where the data subject believes their right to access has not been properly fulfilled. Taking that caveat into account there are generally two types of complaints controllers may be required to manage. Direct complaints made from the data subject to the controller and complaints made to the Data Protection supervisory authority, e.g., the ICO. A data subject should initially make their complaint to the controller and this course of action is typically encouraged by the regulators. However, there will be occasions where the relationship between the data subject and controller has broken down so badly the controller's complaints process is bypassed, if indeed it existed, and the data subject will go straight to the regulator. So, with that in mind let's look at how we can handle each scenario.

**Data subject makes a complaint direct to the organisation**: Occasionally a data subject will not be happy with an aspect of how their DSAR has been handled. Sometimes the data subject will have found something within the DSAR that gives rise to the complaint, e.g. an employee has made a disparaging remark about their character. Another example could be the DSAR material confirms something else is wrong. It's therefore important data subject complaints are handled as part of an effective complaints management process that ensures all the relevant stakeholders are involved as required. If you don't have a complaints procedure already, we recommend you put one in place. In the meantime, you should at the very least have two key pieces of communication - an acknowledgement of the complaint and a response to the complaint itself. Figure 32 shows an example of the initial complaint acknowledgement letter.

Dear **[Name]**,

*[Insert Ref]* **– Data Subject Complaint**

We're sorry you've had cause to complain but thank you for raising your concerns.

In response to your complaint, I will:

- Carry out a thorough and impartial investigation

- Keep you updated on the progress of your complaint

- Work to resolve the complaint as quickly as possible

- Provide a written response within 30 days of this letter

If we have been unable to resolve your complaint within 30 days, you may wish to refer your complaint to the Data Protection Regulator. You can find further information on their website [insert information for relevant Data Protection Regulator].

If you are amenable we can contact you by phone to discuss the matter. Please let us know a number we can call you on and a good time to call.

If you have any questions about the progress of your complaint, please do not hesitate to get in touch.

Yours sincerely

**[Signature Block]**

*Figure 33 - Complaint Acknowledgement Letter*

In figure 34 is an example of a complaint response letter where the controller has got something wrong:

Dear **[Name]**,

*[Insert Ref]* **– Data Subject Complaint**

Thank you for bringing to our attention the incorrect data we have stored in our systems.

On behalf of the company, I would like to sincerely apologise that we did not correct your data when you originally brought this to the attention of a customer service agent and that it took a formal subject access request to resolve the data error. We also understand how frustrating this has been and have taken steps to improve our customer service agent training so similar issues can be handled more efficiently in the future,

We trust that this is a satisfactory response to your complaint and will bring this matter to a close. However, if you wish to discuss this matter further, please let us know how best to contact you.

Yours sincerely

**[Signature Block]**

*Figure 34 - Complaint Response where controller has erred.*

In figure 35 is an example of a complaint response letter where the data subject's complaint is deemed to be without merit.

---

Dear **[Name]**,

**Data Subject Complaint – *[Insert Ref]***

In relation to the aforementioned complaint. We believe the complaint is without merit and we will not be providing any further material.

We have provided copies of the personal data we hold within the statutory deadline, and supplementary information has been provided as required, we believe that you misinterpreted the law for the reasons stated in the next paragraph.

*[You made a request for information to which you are not entitled. Your request was for documents and recordings relating to all business meetings you attended in the course of your employment. The content of those meetings contains your personal data to the limited extent of recording your attendance at those meetings and your contributions to the business issues at those meetings. The content of those meetings is confidential in nature and relates to ongoing business operations. These meetings do not relate to you directly or indirectly. Where a meeting directly or indirectly relates to you directly, and is not covered by an exemption, copies of these artefacts have been provided.]*

We trust that this is a satisfactory response to your complaint, and we now consider the matter closed. If we have been unable to resolve your complaint you may wish to refer the matter to the Data Protection Regulator. You can find further information on their website [insert information for relevant Data Protection Regulator].

Yours sincerely,

**[Signature Block]**"

---

*Figure 35 - Complaint Response Where DS Complaint Is Without Merit*

**Data subject makes a complaint to the Supervisory Authority**: Unfortunately there will be times when a controller cannot resolve a complaint directly with the data subject. At this point the data subject may choose to make a complaint to the supervisory authority. If you have followed the guidance within this book these should be very rare. However, even when a controller has done everything correctly, a data subject may still feel they are entitled to further information.

Where a data subject has made a complaint to a supervisory authority, they should first ask the data subject whether they have attempted to raise their complaint with the controller. If not, the supervisory authority will direct the data subject to give the controller the opportunity to resolve the issue. If, however, the complaint was made and remains unresolved, the supervisory authority may decide to open an investigation. At this point a controller will need to defend the way they have handled the DSAR. It's worth noting a failure to adequately defend a complaint could lead to various forms of enforcement action – so don't just ignore it!

As discussed in chapter one the supervisory authority, in the EU/UK at least, have certain statutory powers. The supervisory authority may choose to provide the controller with an information notice, for example, highlighting to a controller they have misinterpreted the law and failed to process a DSAR correctly. A further escalation could be enforcement, for example, the supervisory authority may compel the controller to provide the data subject with the previously withheld information if the controller has mistakenly withheld but is still unwilling to provide material to the data subject. Such situations are common where documents may highlight some other legal exposure, e.g. discrimination in an employment context. Where the supervisory authority identifies wider systemic issues in a controller's data protection controls, they may choose to conduct an assessment on the controller. Naturally, if you are reading this chapter and have implemented the steps in prior chapters this type of assessment will be a breeze. However, it will be an unnecessary headache and will require resources to be redirected from other tasks – so best avoided if at all possible!

Should you receive communication from the supervisory authority relating to a data subject complaint here is an example of how you may wish to respond. In figure 36 a data subject is asking for information to which they are not entitled.

---

"Dear *[Insert Point of Contact at Supervisory Authority's Name]*,

**Data Subject Complaint – *[Insert ICO Case Ref]***

We write in relation to the above complaint as we believe the data subject's complaint is without merit.

The data subject has been provided copies of the personal data we hold within the statutory deadline; supplementary information has been provided as required and we believe the data subject has erred in their interpretation of the law for the reasons stated in the next paragraph.

*[The data subject has made a request for information to which they are not entitled. The data subject has made a request for documents and recordings relating to all business meetings they attended in the course of their employment. The content of those meetings contains the data subject's personal data to the limited extent of recording their attendance at those meetings and any contribution the data subject made. The controller has provided a written response to this effect. The content of those meetings however is confidential in nature and relates to ongoing business operations. These*

*meetings do not relate to the data subject directly or indirectly. Where a meeting directly or indirectly relates to the data subject, and is not covered by an exemption, copies of these artefacts have been provided.] ***

I hope this provides a satisfactory response to your investigation and we look forward to any guidance you can provide us in resolving the data subject's complaint.

Yours sincerely,

**[Signature Block]**"

*\*replace this section with your own reasons for any actions you have taken in relation to a specific DSAR complaint. But make sure you provide justification for your actions.*

*Figure 36 - Response to Regulator where DS Complaint Is Without Merit*

So, there you have it, by implementing a secure communication mechanism, effective communication management and preparing templates for the predictable exchanges a controller is likely to have with a data subject or their representatives, you should be able to significantly reduce the amount of effort required. We can't stress how important it is to get the communication stage right both in setting the right tone and making sure key information is not accidentally missed.

# Feedback

You have made it to the final section of the final chapter. Wherever you started from to get to this point well done for making it this far! In this section we are going to discuss feedback. If you recall from Chapter 4 we discussed the topic of continual improvement at a high level, but for any continual improvement to occur we need to build feedback mechanisms into our DSAR process. In this section we will be discussing feedback in the context of continual improvement. It's importance and benefits, feedback mechanisms and how to use them to not only make improvements to the DSAR process but also to influence improvements in a wider business context – which in turn should also aid in reducing the overall burden of data protection compliance held by a controller.

Feedback is an essential part of the DSAR process, primarily because it helps a controller understand how well it is doing in complying with its data protection obligations, how well it is able to adapt to changes in those obligations and, from a commercial perspective, how effectively it is using the finite, and often competing, resources assigned to data protection activities. Basically, feedback mechanisms allow a controller to work smart! Anecdotally feedback is often overlooked in the DSAR process. Even in 2023, five years from the EU GDPR coming into force, we still see inaccurate material provided to data subjects relating to the DSAR process. Material that references outdated legislation like the DPA 1998; that requests an upfront fee when charging fees is typically prohibited; or that states requests must be sent in writing to a postal address when requests can be made electronically.

At some point all this material was accurate but it would appear no one at these controller organisations has been keeping up with changes in data protection in recent years. In short, they have not implemented effective feedback mechanisms into their DSAR processes - and if they have not implemented effective feedback mechanisms into their DSAR processes, it's quite possible the same applies for their wider data protection programme! So, how can controllers avoid falling foul of running outdated DSAR processes? How can controllers implement feedback mechanisms to avoid a situation where their processes are no longer compliant with the law?

At a very high level, a great option is for a controller to implement, and possibly certify to, a quality management standard such as ISO 9001 and incorporate their DSAR processes within a wider Quality Management System (QMS). However, implementing a QMS across a whole organisation is not a simple task and is probably (or more likely definitely) outside the scope of a data protection practitioner's remit. That doesn't mean that DSAR processes can't be implemented in a way that embeds the principles of quality management and as you read on, that's exactly what we're going to run through. We'll essentially apply quality management "lite" to the DSAR process.

Our quality management lite framework lite looks like this:

- Horizon Scanning
- Document Control
- Process Control & Monitoring
- Audit

Let's have a look at each of these components in more detail.


## Horizon Scanning

A common misconception with regulation is that once a regulation is codified then it can only be interpreted in one way. This is a naïve viewpoint. Data protection regulations, like many other legal documents, are typically written in general terms, as otherwise they would not be able cater for every possible situation that might occur. In practice data protection regulations are first interpreted by controllers who apply the regulations to their specific circumstances. In the event a data subject complains to a regulator that a controller has processed their data unlawfully the regulator will interpret the regulation themselves and determine whether the controller has acted correctly. If the regulator believes the controller has made an error, they may decide to initiate enforcement action.

Now, this doesn't mean the controller is wrong. Should the controller believe the regulator is mistaken they may choose to hire expensive lawyers to test the controller's interpretation of the regulation in an applicable court, potentially all the way up to a high-level court such as the Court of Justice of the European Union (CJEU). After a lot of money has been spent a precedent will be set which will clarify what is meant by a particular, and often narrow, aspect of the legislation. A good example of this process in the context of DSARs is the case of FSA v Durant which clarified what is meant by the term "relevant filing system". Similarly, where enforcement action is not appealed the content of the enforcement action can also clarify how data protection regulation should be interpreted going forward. In addition to case law and enforcement notices regulators also issue detailed guidance on their websites. As you can imagine this material is constantly changing, so it's important for organisations to conduct horizon scanning to periodically check if anything has altered, and then take appropriate action to update their internal processes.

Horizon scanning can take several forms. At its simplest it could be a periodical internet search using a term like "What's new in data protection?". A practitioner could diarise a few hours a month and make notes of anything that comes up they feel is significant. Another option is to sign up to a data protection newsletter. Most data protection regulators, and many law firms, have a free newsletter that tend to give you good general information. Regulator newsletters tend to focus on national level content though so it's also worth signing up to newsletters from a few different countries if you want to get a wider perspective – especially if you operate across multiple jurisdictions. If you're looking for up-to-date case law this is widely available, however for interpretation and analysis you may find you need to use a paid subscription service, e.g., LexisNexis or Westlaw. Another option for horizon scanning is to join relevant data protection social media groups. Bear in mind with any social media content interpretation by commentators is often subjective and frequently inaccurate. Just because a lot of people like an answer given doesn't mean it is any more accurate either. A final option is to hire an outsourced data protection service that can monitor changes to data protection regulation for you and let you know if you need to make any changes to your processes. Whichever option you choose, when you uncover new guidance, a change in case law or a new piece of analysis, someone in your organisation needs to read it, assess its impact, brief the relevant stakeholders and, where necessary, take appropriate action.

## Document Control

As you have worked your way through this book you will have identified there are several documents and templates you need to maintain. To do this efficiently you are going to need to employ some document control. The main reason document control is important is because it helps ensure accuracy and consistency. Remember our earlier example of material being sent to a data subject with outdated information? You don't want this happening to you! Document control is also helpful for document retrieval and collaboration. If everyone involved in the review process knows where to find documents, and everyone is working on a common version, processes are going to be far more efficient. So, what are some good document control practices? Here are some things to consider:

- Have a consistent document control policy that is applied across the whole organisation
- Every document should have an owner responsible for maintaining the document's accuracy
- All documents, including templates, should be version controlled with older versions withdrawn from circulation
- All documents should be periodically reviewed against a checklist of items relevant to the content of the document
- Where possible templates should be employed for repeated content
- Documents should be easily available from a central repository and making local copies should be discouraged
- Master copies of documents and templates should be archived and access controlled
- Backups should be made to protect against accidental or malicious deletion/modification

The key takeaway for document control is that your DSAR material is a set of living documents. These documents need maintenance, they are not something that gets written and then never reviewed or updated ever again. Even if you bought a template pack or commissioned an external consultant to produce the material for you, maintenance is necessary, and the material needs to be periodically reviewed.

## Process Control & Monitoring

Process control differs from document control. Instead of implementing steps to maintain the accuracy and completeness of your DSAR material, process control requires a controller to implement steps to monitor and manage the effectiveness of each of the DSAR processes described within the RAFM – and good process control is important because uncontrolled processes often have unintended effects that reduce the effectiveness of a process in the pursuit of "efficiency". There are many examples of organisations implementing highly efficient processes that do something very bad but in a very efficient way. Examples include highly efficient supply chains that only use one supplier, a problem then arises when  a war or pandemic erupts in the supplier's country, and they are then unable to supply the components. Perhaps overly complex tools are bought in to automate processes but fail because no one knows how to use them, or maybe the dreaded website chatbots, designed to improve customer service, but instead cause customers to scream into their monitors in frustration as they get caught in an infinite loop – although we're 100% confident ChatGPT and similar models will completely solve that problem…or not.

DSAR processes are not immune from similar misguided attempts by controllers to bring about efficiencies. controllers may implement online forms to speed up their DSAR process but then fail to educate their customer service representatives that the form is only optional. This increases the volume of complaints and increases the effort needed to maintain multiple processes. controllers could implement complicated encryption and hashing processes which require end users to install additional software on their machines. If they fail to appreciate that many of their data subjects do not have the technical capability, or appropriate hardware to decrypt their personal data, they will then be flooded with support enquiries. In many cases the lack of process control has meant the root cause of the perceived problem has been totally misunderstood, and in some cases, vendor salespeople have sold organisations solutions that are simply not fit for purpose. So, how can controllers get process control right? Here are some more top tips:

- Document your processes using an industry standard format such as Business Process Model & Notation (BPMN) - this will reduce the learning curve for those you employ to help you improve your processes, e.g., business analysts or Six Sigma specialists
- Identify appropriate metrics throughout your DSAR processes and collect information at regular intervals - don't just think about the processes you control directly but also consider metrics related to the work other teams do to support the DSAR

- Analyse processes and metrics using different techniques that will help identify the true root cause of bottlenecks, complaints, and inefficiencies - Kaizen, Value Stream Mapping Business Process Re-engineering and the 5-Whys approach are all effective in helping process owners understand fundamental root causes
- Challenge your assumptions and seek wide stakeholder feedback, very few people appreciate being forced to go through a complex process to make a DSAR

There are times where controllers might want to increase inefficiency in their processes in order to slow things down. This may be because the controller is experiencing a higher volume of DSARs than they can physically cope with. Remember, high volumes of DSARs are an indicator in themselves of a broken process elsewhere. It is therefore important that, whilst most DSAR metrics will be for the internal consumption of the person managing the DSAR processes, some metrics should also be reported to senior management. This is to ensure any systemic issues are resolved. Not all metrics are directly related to the DSAR process, but they all give an indication of how well a controller is doing in terms of its right of access obligations and where there are opportunities for improvement. Examples of some metrics that could be useful to practitioners and senior management are:

**Outcomes**: This metric will provide a count of the outcomes of DSARs. Possible outcomes might include the following: -

- Not Fulfilled - Failed ID Checks
- Not Fulfilled - Excessive Request
- Fulfilled – No Further Action
- Fulfilled – Data Subject Challenged
- Fulfilled – Regulatory Complaint
- Fulfilled - Resulted in Legal Action

Understanding the outcome of DSARs will help identify where there are unresolved issues such as an overly complex identification process or a need to provide training to staff to reduce legal exposure.

**Proactive Disclosures**: This metric will provide a count of DSARs where the Data Subject makes a DSAR when they already have access to the personal data, e.g. through a portal or a feature in an application they already use. For organisations that have thousands, if not millions of customers, identifying solutions to support self-service DSARs, even if only partial, could significantly reduce the DSAR burden. Even if you have made the material available for self-service the metric is useful to understand whether your customers know how to access this information or whether help or user interface/experience improvements are needed.

**DSAR Volumes**: This metric provides a count of DSARs made to a controller. It may also be useful to break this down further by placing Data Subjects into categories such as public, customer, patient, employee etc. This metric, when considered with other metrics, seeks to understand where DSARs are coming from. This will allow further investigation to be conducted on how to reduce volumes to as low as possible e.g., by making more data available via a self-service mechanism.

**Exemptions Rejection**: This metric provides a count of how many times an exemption has been incorrectly applied and, as a result, has been overturned either upon internal review or because of regulatory enforcement. This metric can help controllers better understand whether exemptions are being applied correctly or whether further training is required.

**Complaints / Appeals**: The metric is similar to the outcomes metric but with a narrower focus on DSARs that have resulted in complaints or appeals. Understanding the root cause and validity of complaints and appeals can aid in improving your DSAR processes. Another metric that may also be worth considering is to include in your organisation's complaints metrics the number of complaints or appeals that subsequently result in a DSAR. This can help organisations identify issues in their customer service processes to reduce the likelihood of a complaint becoming a DSAR.

**Average Time to Respond**: This metric provides the average number of days it takes for an organisation to respond to a DSAR. This metric could also be broken down into the subsequent stages of the RAFM phases. This can assist a controller in understanding how long each stage takes which, in turn, can aid in focussing improvement efforts on the areas that are taking the longest to complete. This metric is particularly important to ensure that a controller is meeting their regulatory obligations and fulfilling the DSAR within the required regulatory deadline.

**DSAR Cost**: This metric calculates the total cost of fulfilling a DSAR. The way to calculate this will depend on the organisation but could be broken down into the hours taken to complete each task multiplied by an hourly rate per person involved. Additional costs for specialised tools or external services, e.g., legal advice, could also be factored in and then divided by the amount of DSARs received. Understanding the true cost of fulfilling DSARs can help a controller understand whether the cost to the organisation overall could be reduced by making investments elsewhere in the business.

**DSAR Data Size (Initial and Final)**: This metric compares the total file size of your DSAR material when first collected with the total file size at the point of delivery. This can give organisations a better understanding of the sheer volume of data involved and the effort required to consolidate it down to the final amount communicated to the data subject.

**Average Volume of Messages**: This is a similar metric to the DSAR Data Size metric but focuses on message volumes. Message volumes can be extremely high when dealing with employee DSARs. Especially when the employee has been with an organisation for a long time or when their name is somehow tied together with a form of regular reporting. This metric can therefore help organisations understand how well they are applying the data protection principles of data minimisation and storage limitation.

The above list of metrics is not exhaustive but it's also not a mandatory set of metrics that every organisation should be tracking. Each controller will have different challenges and so should pick the metrics that will best help them solve the challenges they uniquely face. The most important point is to ensure that whatever metrics you do collect are collected consistently, accurately and drive appropriate action. If a metric is not driving action, then it's probably not the right metric to track. As a final word on metrics, don't be afraid to drop metrics that never change, or reduce the frequency of collection, in favour of collecting a wider suite of metrics.

## Audit

The final stage of our quality management "lite" is audit. Audit in this context is the commissioning of an independent body to come and assess your DSAR processes against a good practice guide – like this one! An audit can take many forms. It could be a formal audit organised as part of your organisations normal audit schedule, it could be an internal peer review where someone from a different part of the business kicks the tyres on what you say you do on paper compared to what happens in practice, or it could be an external review from a company that provides such services. Whichever approach is chosen the key is to make sure the audit is properly scoped, the findings are supported by evidence, and the auditor is competent to conduct an effective audit. Audits can strike fear into many people as they worry they are going to be presented in a bad light should the audit find deficiencies. This is one of the reasons why the culture aspect of the RAFM is so important. If the organisation has a culture of learning and improvement there should be little to worry about when it comes to being audited.

And that's a wrap for feedback. Hopefully this all seems like common sense, but we've consciously included feedback in the model because it is often treated as an afterthought or is overlooked completely. Even if you can't implement an organisation-wide Quality Management System, or you can't implement all the stages of the "lite" version described in this section, it's still worth collecting metrics and doing some basic horizon scanning.

# Summary

You have now reached the end of the book. Thank you so much for taking the time to work your way through the content. We hope this book has provided a comprehensive guide to effectively managing and responding to Data Subject Access Requests (DSARs) under the whichever data protection legislation you are required to follow. Each chapter has focused on a specific aspect of DSAR management, providing key points and practical advice for controllers to maintain compliance and foster a transparent data protection culture. Let's review each chapter in turn and their key takeaways.

In chapter one we discussed data protection principles, data subjects' rights, and DSAR recognition. The key takeaways were understanding the principles, recognizing various ways a DSAR can be made and the typical 30-day compliance timeframe.

In chapter two we discussed Articles 25, 30, and 35 of the GDPR and their implications on handling DSARs. The key takeaways were the roles of Data Protection by Design and Default, Data Protection Impact Assessments, and Record of Processing Activities in reducing DSAR effort.

We then moved on to chapter three where we discussed the Right to Access Fulfilment Model (RAFM) and its origins. It was in this chapter we learned that the RAFM provides us with the structured approach needed to fulfil DSARs consistently and accurately. We discovered the RAFM consists of a central 'Accountability' hub and learned the four iterative phases of preparation, collection, treatment, and delivery.

In chapter four we discussed accountability and its integration into the RAFM. The key takeaway was the importance of leadership, transparency, organisational culture, and the need for continuous improvement when implementing the RAFM.

In chapter five we discussed the preparation phase. The key takeaways were the need for appropriate resources, effective training and to deploy case management software to help reduce the administrative burden of your DSAR processes.

In chapter six we discussed the collection phase. The key takeaways were the need to implement processes to verify the data subject and the nature of the material they wish to access, search strategies and preservation of collected material to ensure accurate and efficient processing of DSARs.

In chapter seven we discussed the treatment phase. The key takeaways were the need to understand how to review material to remove duplication; the need to understand when exemptions apply, and when they do not; the importance of getting redaction right and what needs to be included in the DSAR material, so it is complete when sent to the data subject.

In the final chapter we discussed the communication phase. The key takeaways were the importance of controllers having clear and effective communication processes that build trust with individuals whose personal data they hold. We also looked at the need for controllers to build feedback mechanisms into their DSAR processes to ensure they are being effectively managed.

And there you have it! All you need to manage the DSARs that are made to your organisation..

Once again, thanks for taking the time to read our book and we hope you got something useful out of these pages.

Good luck out there!

# Glossary

The following definitions are useful to the understanding the Right to Access Fulfilment Model as it sits within a data protection legislative framework. The glossary is not exhaustive and key terms will also be described and discussed throughout the book.

**Child**: For the purposes of GDPR is a Natural person who requires parental consent, usually if they are below 16. EU Member States can, however, reduce the requirement for consent to those no younger than 13 (i.e. if the Natural Person is over 13, parental consent would not be required).

**Consent**: any freely given, specific, informed, and unambiguous indication of the data subject's wishes by which he or she, by a statement or by a clear affirmative action, signifies agreement to the processing of personal data relating to him or her.

**controller**: the natural or legal person, public authority, agency, or other body which, alone or jointly with others, determines the purposes and means of the processing of personal data; where the purposes and means of such processing are determined by Union or Member State law, the controller or the specific criteria for its nomination may be provided for by Union or Member State law.

**Data Protection Impact Assessment (DPIA)**: An assessment of the impact of the envisaged processing operations on the protection of personal data and the rights and freedoms of natural persons.

**Data Subject**: A Natural Person whose personal data is processed by a controller or processor.

**Data Subject Rights**: The legal rights of individuals with regard to their personal data, including the right to access, rectify, erase, restrict processing, object to processing, and data portability.

**Data Subject Access Request (DSAR)**: A request, made by a natural person, to access personal data held by a controller or processor,

**Data Protection Officer (DPO)**: a person with expert knowledge of data protection law and practices who assists the controller or processor to monitor internal compliance with GDPR. Such data protection officers, whether or not they are an employee of the controller, should be in a position to perform their duties and tasks in an independent manner.

**Encryption**: The process of encoding data to protect its confidentiality, typically by converting it into a code to prevent unauthorized access.

**Information Security**: The protection of information and information systems from unauthorised access, use, disclosure, disruption, modification, or destruction in order to provide confidentiality, integrity, and availability.

**Natural Person**: Essentially an EU citizen who is alive. A Natural Person may also be referred to as a data subject.

**Personal Data**: any information relating to an identified or identifiable Natural Person (or 'data subject'); an identifiable Natural Person is one who can be identified, directly or indirectly, in particular by reference to an identifier such as a name, an identification number, location data, an online identifier, or to one or more factors specific to the physical, physiological, genetic, mental, economic, cultural, or social identity of that Natural Person.

**Personal Data Breach**: a breach of security leading to the accidental or unlawful destruction, loss, alteration, unauthorised disclosure of, or access to, personal data transmitted, stored, or otherwise processed.

**Processing**: any operation or set of operations, which is performed on personal data or on sets of personal data, whether or not by automated means, such as collection, recording, organisation, structuring, storage, adaptation or alteration, retrieval, consultation, use, disclosure by transmission, dissemination or otherwise making available, alignment or combination, restriction, erasure, or destruction.

**Profiling**: any form of automated processing of personal data consisting of the use of personal data to evaluate certain personal aspects relating to a Natural Person, in particular, to analyse or predict aspects concerning that Natural Person's performance at work, economic situation, health, personal preferences, interests, reliability, behaviour, location or movements.

**processor**: a natural or legal person, public authority, agency, or other body which processes personal data on behalf of the controller.

**Sensitive Data**: special categories of information relating to an identified or identifiable Natural Person (or 'data subject'). Examples include racial or ethnic origin, political opinions, religious or philosophical beliefs, or trade union membership, genetic data, biometric data, sex life or sexual orientation.

**Supervisory Authority**: the regulator within a European country who will provide regulatory oversight for GDPR, provide guidance and advice and, where necessary impose corrective actions or administrative fines.

**Third Country**: any country which is not an EU Member State (e.g. UK USA, India, China, or the Philippines)

# Index

# About the Authors

Stephen Massey is a Data Protection and Information Security Practitioner with a career spanning over 20 years. Stephen has also authored the best-selling Ultimate GDPR Practitioner Guide now in its second edition. Stephen is currently researching his PhD at Birmingham University in the UK and holds an IAPP Fellow of Information Privacy in good standing.

When not writing and consulting, Stephen loves nothing more than to spend time with his family. Stephen also enjoys skiing and SCUBA diving.

Catriona Leafe has over 20 years of experience in HR Administration and Education. Most recently as the Training & Development Manager at Fox Red Risk, working alongside Stephen. Catriona holds a A (Hons) in Tourism Management at Coventry University.

When not writing and developing training material, Catriona loves to escape to the coast with the windswept beaches of northern Scotland being her absolute favourite

Printed in Great Britain
by Amazon

46522860R00104